# PROMISE AND AND DELIVERANCE

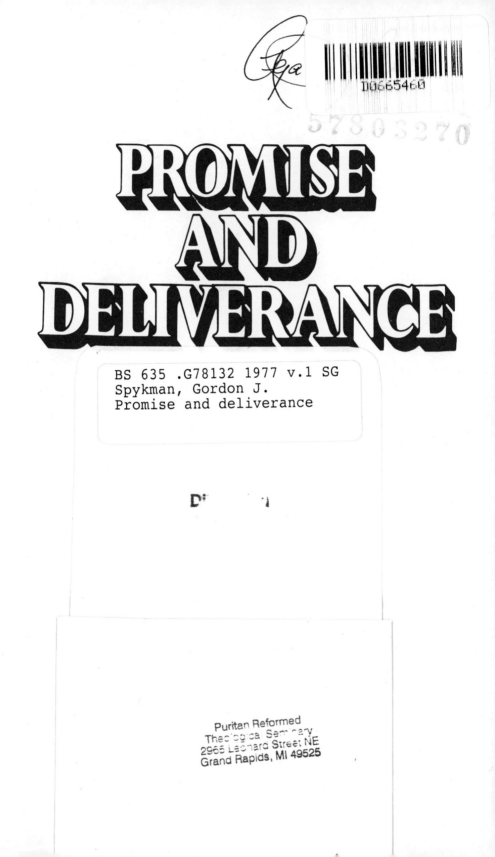

GORDON J. SPYKMAN

VOLUME I
FROM CREATION TO THE CONQUEST
OF CANAAN

STUDY GUIDE

PAIDEIA PRESS
St. Catharines, Ontario, Canada
1977

ISBN 0-88815-005-9
Printed in the United States of America.

BS635G78132 1977

v i
study guide

# Preface

John Calvin introduces his classic work, *The Institutes of the Christian Religion*, as a "necessary tool" to prepare and instruct the reader "for the reading of the divine Word," so that "it will not be difficult for him to determine what he ought especially to seek in Scripture, and to what end he ought to relate its contents."

De Graaf's monumental work *Promise and Deliverance* is meant to play a similar role in the life of the Christian community. It should be viewed not as a substitute for searching the Scriptures but as an aid designed to help us understand more fully and clearly the meaning of the Biblical message. Its central unifying theme is the unfolding drama of covenant history. Retracing De Graaf's steps through the Bible has been an eye-opening experience for countless Dutch readers. Now that the book is available in English, it can render even greater service as we learn to read, interpret, and incorporate into our daily living Scripture's ongoing witness to God's redeeming work in Jesus Christ.

This little handbook is nothing more than a companion volume to De Graaf's book. Therefore it cannot stand alone. As a study guide, it is intended to play a servant role in bringing into sharper focus the story of the Bible as retold by De Graaf. For the sake of easy cross-reference, it follows the format of De Graaf's own book in its chapter titles and numbers. The questions also follow generally the sequence of thought as developed in each chapter.

I have written this study guide in the hope that it will help bring the truth of Scripture closer to the readers via De Graaf's work. More specifically, this study guide is written with a large cross section of the Christian community in mind. It is aimed at students and teachers in Bible classes, leaders and participants in Bible discussion clubs, families that take time to reflect seriously upon the Scriptures, pastors and their parishioners in church groups, those who engage in personal Bible study, and all others who wish to search out the meaning of God's Word as a lamp to their feet and a light upon their path.

I hope that those who use this study guide will find that it helps them attain a richer grasp of the message of God's Word.

# 1: The Kingdom of God

*Genesis 1—2:3*

1. God's Kingdom encompasses the entire creation. *Everything* He has made is part of that Kingdom. What tasks are included in "kingdom service"? Is there any limit to kingdom service? Does *your* work fall within the scope of kingdom service?

2. Man is the crown of creation (p.33). Just what is man's special task in relation to everything else God made? Is our lofty position a reason for feeling proud? Or should we feel called to humble service instead?

3. "For better or worse, the world had been placed in man's hands" (p. 34). Are we truly responsible for the world's destiny? Can't we shrug our shoulders when things go wrong and declare, "It was God's will"?

4. God gave man dominion over all He had made. Does this "dominion" give us the right to exploit the resources of creation? What can we do to exercise faithful stewardship over the good gifts of God's creation? Why should we preserve the creation carefully if it is destined to be replaced by a new world or renewed world?

5. God carried out the work of creation in a six-day framework. Is the order in the creation story also a reason for us to strive for order and system as we go about our work? When man exercises dominion over the earth, can he count on things falling into place automatically? Or does man have a responsibility to see to it that there is order in the world he governs in God's place? How does this issue apply to the protection of endangered species, for example?

6. Why did the creation week need that seventh day? In other words, what does the sabbath have to do with creation and with our work in this world? How does God's sabbath rest, which He allows us to share, enrich our life in His Kingdom?

7. De Graaf emphasizes that God *takes pleasure* in the works of His hands (p. 34). Does He want us to share in that pleasure? If God takes delight even in seemingly insignificant creatures, are we justified in doing as we please with such creatures?

8. Is the creation story recorded in Genesis God-centered or Christ-centered? (See John 1:1-3 and Colossians 1:15-20.) Was the Holy Spirit also at work in creation? Can we read the Bible as pointing to Christ from Genesis 1 through Revelation 22?

## 2: The Covenant of God's Favor

*Genesis 2:4-25*

1. Chapter 1 presents creation as the beginning of the Kingdom of God. It also teaches us to look at creation from the perspective of the covenant. How are Kingdom and covenant related? Is the Kingdom somehow larger than the covenant? Or are Kingdom and covenant two ways of looking at our life in God's creation?

2. How are we to understand the Bible's teaching that the *entire creation*—and not just man—stands in a covenant relationship to God? What if there were no covenant connection between God and the world?

3. God makes His covenant with man as the *head* of creation. That covenant involves both promises and obligations. What promises does God make? What claims can we make upon God because of those promises? What are our covenant obligations?

4. We tend to think of the covenant only in connection with covenant children, covenant homes, covenant signs and seals, covenant education. Is such a notion of the covenant too limited? Does covenant living have anything to do with labor, business, civic duties, money, what we read? How big is the Biblical view of the covenant?

5. We often speak of covenant living as partnership with God. What are our aims in that partnership? How can we reflect God's image and give others a glimpse of that image when we carry out the tasks He has assigned to us?

6. De Graaf points out that it is misleading to speak of the covenant of "works" (p. 37). Why? Is the covenant made with Adam (the covenant of "favor") completely separate from the covenant made with Christ (the covenant of "grace")? Or are they two phases in God's single covenant with creation?

7. What is the relationship between the head of the first covenant (Adam) and the Head of the second covenant (Christ)? Is there good Biblical reason for "running ahead of the story" the way De Graaf does? (p. 42). Why talk about Christ when dealing with Old Testament passages that make no direct reference to Him?

8. What was the role of the two special trees in God's original covenant with mankind in Adam? What test were Adam and Eve subjected to when they faced those two trees? What decision did God want them to make? What does the choice they made have to do with us? The image of the tree also appears in God's Final Act (see Rev. 2:7; 22:2, 14). What does this suggest to you about redemption as the renewal of creation?

9. Creation lays the groundwork for everything that has developed in the history of the world. What does this imply for our Christian view of history? Does man create anything truly new in history? Or is he limited to working with the potentials and possibilities that God provided at the very outset? What does this suggest to you about God's control of history? About man as a shaper of history?

10. Creation is God's work. Culture, i.e. the "cultivation" of the earth and all that comes with it, is man's response to creation. Is man ever capable of acting on his own? Or does he need divine direction? What does the cultural mandate mean for life and work in our time? (See Genesis 1:23-8.)

11. Marriages are breaking down all around us. Many people today speak of marriage as a trial arrangement, an experimental relationship that can be terminated by either party at any time. But the Bible calls marriage a *covenant*—the highest creaturely

expression of the covenant God made with mankind. If a marriage is a covenant relationship, under what circumstances can it be terminated? What does covenantal troth and fidelity mean for marriage?

12. How should the partnership of husband and wife come to expression in daily living? Can the man be the head of the home without exercising his authority in a domineering way? How do mutual love and service in marriage fit in with covenant obligations?

# 3: The Covenant of God's Grace

*Genesis 3*

1. As De Graaf points out, the central emphasis in Genesis 3 is on God's renewing grace, not man's fall into sin. Even God's judgment is dealt with in the context of His redemption. What does this tell us about the Bible? Does the Bible focus primarily on man's sin or on God's salvation? On judgment or on redemption? How are these two sides of God's dealings with creation interrelated?

2. Bible scholars have wrestled long and hard with the question of the origin of sin and evil in the world. Should we somehow seek their cause behind the scenes—in the eternal decrees of God or in the arena of spiritual warfare among the angels? Or should we rest content with the rather straightforward historical account of the fall given in Genesis, the account that locates the origin of sin and evil within the realm of the human drama, within our world of experience?

3. How can we best describe the nature of man's original sin? Was it disobedience? Unfaithfulness? Rebellion? Lust for power? Pride? Folly? Or what? Or a combination of all these elements? Are these elements also present in our sinful lives today?

4. What tactics did satan use to infiltrate man's perfect life, draw him away from God, and seduce him into a broken covenantal relationship?

5. The basic choice in man's original sin was between honoring the sovereignty of God and asserting his own autonomy (the sovereignty of man, man as a "law unto himself"). In other words, man had to choose between God's Word as the rule for life and "another word." Is that still the basic choice facing us today? How do these "other words" come through to us in our time? What forms do they take?

6. Can you illustrate the truth that sin is always an illusion, something self-deceptive and disappointing, something that lures us into a make-believe world? That it promises freedom, but leads into bondage? It has been said that "sin brings its own evil rewards." In what sense is this true?

7. Did sin break only the covenantal harmony between God and man? Or did it also shatter the harmony between man and the rest of creation—and the harmony within the community of mankind? What evidences of the broken covenant confront us in our daily newspapers?

8. The old New England Primer used little verses to teach the alphabet. The letter "A" was memorized by means of this rhymed verse: "In Adam's fall we sinned all." How were/are we involved in that original sin? Is it fair on God's part to hold us corporately responsible for Adam's sin? How is our involvement in the first Adam's fall related to our involvement in the redeeming work of the last Adam, Jesus Christ? (See Romans 5.)

9. God's seeking fallen man was an act of both judgment and grace. How are God's acts of judgment and redemption inter-related? How do they come together in His confrontation with Adam and Eve? In our life experience? In Jesus Christ?

# 4: Living Seed

*Genesis 4*

1. Why is it important to recognize that the Bible's central emphasis is on God's speaking and acting—and not on human examples of obedient and/or disobedient responses to God's Word?

Making human response the norm for Christian living is often called moralism. What are the weaknesses and dangers of moralizing when dealing with Bible stories?

2. De Graaf points to the Biblical line which runs from Adam, first through Abel, then Seth, to Christ. Explain how this covenantal insight is important for understanding the overall message of the Bible. How do the various geneologies scattered throughout the Bible (Gen. 5, 10, 11; Ruth 4:18-22; I Chron. 1-9; Ezra 2; Matt. 1; Luke 3) contribute to this insight? In what way was Abel both a type and an antitype of the coming promised Messiah?

3. What was the forward-looking, redemptive importance of sacrifice in Old Testament times, beginning already during the lifetime of Adam and Eve? What was the deeply religious difference between Cain and Abel? How did it show up in their sacrifices? Is there any way of explaining such radically opposed responses to God's covenant Word of grace?

4. The Bible often speaks of a "Godly fear," which is the same as faith. But it also speaks of an "ungodly fear," a fear of the Word of God, such as in the life of Cain. Demonstrate how Cain was driven by an "ungodly fear." If faith, then, generates assurance and trust, while fear generates a jittery outlook on life, why is there so much fear even among believers? What does John mean when he says that perfect love casts out fear? (I John 4:18).

5. God gave man the cultural mandate and made man a cultural creature. Hence all men do in fact engage in cultural activities. Did Cain's descendants err in becoming too involved in cultural developments—or by becoming wrongly involved? Should believers be suspicious of cultural enterprises? Why is it that unbelievers are often the ones who take the lead in cultural involvement? Is it possible to place one's trust in cultural achievements instead of in God's Word? How can we help build a Christian culture? Can we make faithful use of the results of unbelievers' activities in their pursuit of the cultural mandate?

6. Scripture is the story of God's covenant faithfulness in the face of man's unfaithfulness. Work out this central theme in terms of the new hope which was born with Seth after the death of Abel and the downfall of Cain. Life out of death—how is this

Biblical focus developed throughout the Old Testament? How is it fulfilled in Christ? How does it come to expression today?

7. In creation already God provided for a weekly sabbath, for refreshment and renewal. In the days of Enosh, communal worship services apparently began. Under Moses, Israel's sabbath life was further developed. Christ is the fulfillment of the sabbath law. The New Testament Church gathered for worship on the Lord's day. What is the relationship between Sunday and the sabbath? What is the meaning of the New Testament sabbath? How should we observe it? Though the forms of worship change, what is the abiding and normative place of worship in the Christian life?

# 5: Saved by Water

*Genesis 6-9*

1. When we discuss the flood, we usually speak of God *destroying* the world by the flood. In De Graaf, however, the Biblical emphasis falls on God *saving* the world by water. Are these two viewpoints contradictory? Or does the flood reveal both God's judgment and His redemption? How are these two acts of God interrelated? Is it true that salvation is God's last word, and judgment His second last word? How can judgment be a means unto the end of redemption?

2. Explain how the covenant of nature God made with Noah is a further development in the historical unfolding of the covenant of grace revealed to Adam and anchored in Christ.

3. We sometimes talk about growing in grace. But sinfulness also undergoes an historical process of growth—until it is ripe for judgment. Indicate the ways in which this growing apostasy had taken place among the ancestors and contemporaries of Noah.

4. How are we to understand that God saved the world by water through believing Noah, thus preserving His creation—and all this for the sake of Christ? How can we read this passage in a Christ-centered way? In what sense is Noah a type of Christ?

How does the flood signify baptism? How does it reflect the final judgment?

5. How does Noah's preaching concerning the coming judgment reflect the "foolishness of the gospel"? Can the same be said of the Church's witness to Christ's final coming in judgment? Is that notion also foolishness to the world around us?

6. When God saved the world by water, He revealed His concern for His creation. As De Graaf points out, Noah, too, loved God's earth and wanted it saved. Is it wrong for believers to love God's good earth? How can we show that we care about God's creation? What can we do to develop a down-to-earth Christian life-style?

7. At this new beginning in the world's history, Noah responded to God's covenant claim upon him by offering a sacrifice of dedication *before* going forth eagerly to re-develop the potentials of creation and cultivate the earth anew. His work began with worship. What does this suggest concerning the relationship of worship and work in our lives? Does our week begin with worship or end with worship?

8. In the light of God's covenant promises made to Noah, may we go forward in the confidence that God will never again radically interrupt the development of world history until the end comes? How did God confirm that promise? Can this assurance of continuity, this assurance that world history will run its course to the end, become the occasion for spiritual complacency? (See II Peter 3:1-7.)

# 6: The Emergence of Distinct Peoples

*Genesis 11:1-9*

1. In Noah's day the world had been saved by water. Yet water itself cannot bring salvation. It was only a symbol of the real salvation which was to come. At the time of the tower of Babel, God's great act of salvation was still a future hope. People were still living without faith in the promised Messiah. Illustrate this by sketching the sinful human situation at the time of the Babel.

2. Note how De Graaf repeatedly describes sinful human strivings as motivated by *fear* as opposed to *faith* (pp. 68-9). What form did such fear take at Babel? Are we who live after the coming of Christ also driven at times by fear instead of faith? How does this show up in our lives?

3. There is a motto which goes like this: "In unity lies strength." Is unity among men always wrong? Is it always right? What is the difference between true unity and false unity? What are the false unities that people rely on today, even after the unifying work of Christ? A powerful state? A strong economy? Belonging to the same social class (class struggle)? Common interests? Political parties? Labor unions? Alumni associations?

4. Man is created to live in community. Individualism is a sinful illusion. What forms of communal life should we seek to encourage in our day? Is setting up communities in separation from society always wrong? Is it always right?

5. In God's covenantal plan for mankind which unfolds through the Old and New Testament history of salvation, the repeated strivings toward a false unity, such as at Babel, were finally fulfilled in the coming of Christ. How was Pentecost God's answer to the problems raised at Babel?

6. At Babel the parting of the ways came about over the question of language. How important is a common language as a key to the religious and cultural identity of a people? Did the true spiritual unity present in the New Testament church set aside differences in language? Did it break through and cross over language barriers? Should we support the movement to make Esperanto or some other language the international language? Are language differences sufficient cause for the existence of separate churches or states?

7. God wants unity among men. Yet, at Babel He brings about sharp diversities. Why? To counteract man's drive toward solidarity in a sinful way of life? Are the diversities among peoples today a means in God's hand to check and curb the accumulation of human power in one place? Is centralization of power always wrong? Should Christians always encourage decentralization of power?

8. How was God's intervention at Babel both a *curse* upon man's rebellion and at the same time a *blessing* for the human race? Are there legitimate and healthy diversities among men which God built into the good order of His creation? Were these being stifled at Babel? Did God's act of dispersing the peoples help to bring the diversity to expression? How should we honor rightful differences among men in race, sex, calling, insight, talents, and so forth? Should we support egalitarian efforts to level out all differences among people, e.g. the unisex movement?

9. Does God's will for human history call for separate national states, each with its own character and culture? Or should we work toward a world-state? Should Christians think in global terms? Are multi-national corporations a renewed effort to build a modern economic tower of Babel? What forms of false outward unity aimed at glorifying human power do you see in the world today? Could such a unity be used to promote the kingdom of the antichrist in opposition to the Kingdom of God in Jesus Christ?

# 7: Blessed in the One

*Genesis 12*

1. Again and again in the Old Testament, God creates "new beginnings" (e.g. with Noah, David, the return from captivity). What is the unique importance of this "new beginning" with Abram?

2. After the scattering of mankind at Babel and the subsequent emergence of *many* peoples, the need of the hour was *one* line leading forward to the fulfillment of God's promises. How is it possible that the covenantal destiny of the world should ride on one man? What was really important in the long run—this single individual named Abram, or his seed? What does Paul mean in saying that the call of Abram reached its climax in "not seeds, as of many, but seed, as of one, namely, Christ Jesus"? (Gal. 3:16).

3. The call of Abram is generally considered to be the first roughly datable event in Old Testament history. Can you give it an approximate date?

4. Abram moved along the Fertile Crescent from one rather highly civilized region, Ur of the Chaldeans, via Haran, to another, the city-states in the land of Canaan, with Egypt lying beyond. Can you picture these cultures of his day?

5. Abram went out from his homeland bound for a new land which God would show him, but he did not know where God would lead him (Heb. 11:8-10). Was this "blind faith"? He had God's Word to go by. Was this enough? Is it so important to know exactly where our ways will lead us, if only we have a reliable Guide? The real test in Abram's life was simply taking God at His Word. Describe the various aspects of this testing experience. What can we learn from what Abram went through?

6. Why is Abraham called "the friend of God"? (James 2:23).

7. Why did God call this particular man, i.e. Abram? Was he better than others, more holy than his pagan fellow men? Or does the emphasis fall on God's electing love looking ahead to the coming Messiah? What more can we say?

8. Why does Matthew trace the line of Christ back to Abraham (Matt. 1), whereas Luke traces it back to Adam (Luke 3)? Is the covenant made with Abram a *new* covenant or a renewal of the covenant going back to Adam?

9. God "separated" Abram for a special role in covenant history. What does spiritual separation mean? Non-involvement in the affairs of the world around us? Or, living life to the full, yet dedicated to God? How can we be *in* the world, yet not *of* it? Does this sometimes demand of us, as of Abram, a radical break with our surroundings?

10. The saving promises made to Abram were very down-to-earth—a seed, a nation, a land, and thus a blessing to the whole world. Does salvation remove us from earthly life or renew us in it?

11. In what sense may *we* (not just the Jews) be called "the children of Abraham"? (Gal. 3:29).

12. The land of promise to which God led Abram stood at the crossroads of the ancient world, at the intersection point of three continents, between the two great civilizations of that time, Mesopotamia and Egypt. What is the importance of this crucial

location for the later history of Israel, and still later, in New Testament times, for the spread of the gospel?

13. The Bible has been called a totally honest book, never white-washing the sins of the saints. How is this clear from its account of how Abram dealt with Sarai in Egypt?

# 8: Christ Alone

*Genesis 13*

1. Why did God concentrate His redeeming purposes on Abram alone rather than on Abram *and* Lot? How is this emphasis on "Abram alone" related to the central Biblical theme of "Christ alone"? How did Abram's "partnership" with Lot, his last link with the past, compromise that redemptive focus?

2. Did God call Abram as a personal favor—or with a view to creating out of him a new people (Israel), and out of that new people the promised Messiah, and in Christ a new community (the Church), and ultimately a new mankind to inhabit a new earth under new heavens? Explain.

3. In the patriarchal stories the Bible attaches great importance to *land,* the land of promise, a land with a future, this piece of land called Canaan. Why this emphasis? Was Canaan merely acreage for tilling soil and herding cattle and gaining a living? Just a piece of real estate? Or was it because God had foreordained that big things were to happen there, redemptive events of cosmic significance i.e. the life and death and resurrection of Jesus Christ? How large is "the promised land" today, after the coming of Christ? As large as the state of Israel? Or is it worldwide? In the light of these considerations, how are we to evaluate the current Zionist movement and the constant Jewish-Arab disputes about Palestine?

4. What was Lot's mistake in seeking to divide the land and choose the better part? What does it mean that he wanted his portion *without* the promise? Is this an ancient form of that modern heresy called "secularism," wanting God's *goods* apart from the *God* who bestows them? Reflect on this line taken from De

Graaf: "A Canaan separate from the promise made to Abram is a Canaan separate from the Christ who would issue from Abram's loins" (p. 85).

5. Abram inherited the land. He possessed it not by deed or title but by faith in the sure promise of God. And he acted accordingly. How was this possible? Does his action also reflect something of what our outlook upon the world should be? "The meek shall inherit the earth" (Matt. 5:5). "All things are yours" (I Cor. 3:21-3).

# 9: Blessed by the Greater

*Genesis 14*

1. Abram was a type of Christ. How did his life point forward to the coming Messiah? In his meeting with Melchizedek, however, he was the lesser of the two. In what sense was Melchizedek the greater? (Ps. 110:4; Heb. 7).

2. The two biggest temptations which believers constantly face are to isolate themselves from the world around them or to accommodate themselves to it. The latter appears to have been the great temptation here. Lot met this temptation in one way, Abram in another. Explain the difference. Is it also true for us that consecration to the will of God is the only true answer to the temptation of accommodation?

3. Melchizedek exercised a priestly office before the house of Aaron was anointed to the priesthood in Israel. Christ fulfilled that priestly office by His once-for-all sacrifice. He now calls us to exercise that priestly office as a means of blessing to the world. How can we exercise it in our day?

4. What is a tithe? What did it mean for Abram to give a tithe to Melchizedek? What was the purpose of the tithe in Israel's history? What form should tithing take in our lives?

5. Why was it important for Abram to keep the doors closed to the Canaanite way of life? Would accepting any part of the loot have made him beholden to them? Wouldn't it have compromised his

stance of total dependence upon the Lord? Was this principle important enough to risk winning their disfavor? Is such faith still a stumbling block to the world? Do we have the courage to live up to this principle today?

6. Abram proposed the separation and agreed to Lot's choice. Yet, at bottom, in the light of God's covenant promise, this was an impossible transaction. Why?

7. Believers may—and sometimes must—struggle to gain a place on the earth. But in what spirit? Upon what basis? And with a view to what goal?

8. Is it not a severe trial of faith for Christians to believe that the whole earth is their promised inheritance in Jesus Christ when, in fact, all the circumstances seem to point in the opposite direction? When their God-given rights as parents, students, workers, and citizens are often denied? How can we cling to Christ's Word that "all authority is mine in heaven and on earth" (Matt. 28:18) in the face of the hard reality that the movements of world history seem to be largely under the control of ungodly powers?

# 10: The Lord in the Covenant

*Genesis 15*

1. In these patriarchal stories we read again and again of God "making covenant" with Abram. Should these encounters be understood as a series of different covenants or as successive steps in the unfolding of the one covenant of grace? How is God's act of "covenanting" with Abram related to His "covenanting" acts with Noah and Adam? Are there basically many covenants or one covenant?

2. Who are the two parties in this covenant which God made with Abram? Are they equal partners? Who takes the initiative? Who is the Head of the Covenant? Who is its Mediator? What is Abram's role in it, and ours? How are we included in the covenant of grace?

3. In the light of Scripture, how are faith and works related to each

other? Is faith a work which merits God's favor or reward? Or is it a gift of God's grace? Is it active or inactive? How does faith work?

4. What does it mean that "the Lord was Abram's righteousness"? (p. 95). How does Paul reinforce this message in his teaching that Abram's righteousness (justification) and ours is by faith alone? (Rom. 4).

5. Abram was a man of faith. Yet he had to wrestle hard in coming to terms with God's promises. How was his faith being tested? Is there room for doubt in the life of faith?

6. Were God's promises fulfilled completely during Abram's lifetime? During the history of the people of Israel? Or finally and fully in Jesus Christ? How can we share in the promises made to Abram?

7. This vision of Abram's was a revelation from God. But note how divine revelation enters fully into history, making use of the legal customs of the day—the animal halves and the burning torch. What does this teach us about God's ways of revealing Himself? How can revelation be fully historical in form and yet come with a supra-historical message? Can you cite other instances to illustrate this point?

8. The strange things that happened in Abram's vision were signs of the covenant. What signs did God later give Israel to confirm the covenant? What signs of God's covenant promises do we have today?

9. Does the strength of the covenant depend ultimately on our faithfulness or God's? What if it depended on ours? What role, then, does our faithfulness play?

# 11: God Hears

1. Why is it important to recognize that the central concern in this Bible story is not Hagar, nor Sarai, nor even Abram, but the covenant promise? What happens if we treat the history of Hagar and Ishmael as a separate, independent theme?

2. In their dealings with Hagar, Abram and Sarai were acting out of frustration and impatience rather than faith. Is their doubt and unbelief in such circumstances understandable?

3. According to the customs of the day, the child born to Hagar (Ishmael) was to be reckoned as Sarai's child (or more properly, Abram's). How was this possible?

4. What was the nature of the injustice which arose within Abram's tent, within this covenant circle?

5. Explain how God's concern for Hagar and her son was motivated by His forward-looking redemptive purposes centered in Jesus Christ. How was Hagar's link with Abram's household also her link with God's covenant promises?

6. Why such a heavy emphasis on the importance of justice, righteous living and fairness in this story? Why does the judgment of God rest so heavily upon injustice—especially when it prevails among believers? Does this help to explain the recurring call to social justice in Israel by the later prophets? What forms of injustice are Christians called to fight against in our times?

7. Were these tensions within Abram's household the beginnings of present-day hostilities between Jews and Arabs, between Islam and Christianity?

8. Can you describe the humiliation Abram experienced (i.e. God rebuking his weakness of faith) when he was called to name Hagar's son *God hears* (Ishmael)?

9. What are the deeds of faith to which we should be led after reflecting on the questions raised by De Graaf in the final paragraph of this chapter?

# 12: God the Almighty

*Genesis 17*

1. How is the almighty power of the covenant God here revealed in the life of Abram and Sarai? In what sense can this promised birth be called a miracle? What was the deepest level of spiritual experience which this miraculous event brought about in Abram's life? How does circumcision symbolize this miracle of grace?

2. How inclusive was the "seed" (the descendants) which was to come forth from Abram and this promised son? Who are the children of Abram in our time?

3. Does Abram's humble response of faith to God's revelation suggest something about the proper place of worship in the lives of believers?

4. What is the significance of God's changing Abram's name to *Abraham* and Sarai's name to *Sarah*?

5. In what sense is Jesus Christ *the* Son of Abraham? What did Christ Himself say about people who too easily claim that they are children of Abraham? (John 8:31-40). What did John the Baptist say? (Matt. 3:7-10).

6. What was the covenantal meaning of circumcision? How is that same meaning carried over into baptism? How serious is it to reject not only these signs of the covenant but thereby also the riches of the covenant itself?

7. Do we ever have occasion, as Abraham did, to burst out in the joyful laughter of faith at unexpected demonstrations of God's grace in our lives? Do we laugh in delight when we think of God's work of saving His people and His world? Is *Isaac* (laughter) still a fitting name for Christians to bear today?

8. The response of faith to the marvels of God's faithfulness and love is that of childlike obedience. How can we go about displaying such obedience in our day?

# 13: God's Confidant

*Genesis 18*

1. How do the three episodes in this chapter show that God was taking Abraham into His confidence in the unfolding of His covenant purposes?

2. In Bible times, sharing a meal was the most intimate form of fellowship. How is this apparent in the hospitality Abraham showed his heavenly visitors? In this communion around his table, how did Abraham demonstrate his servant role in the covenant? How does that scene point forward to the time when the Son of God would eat and drink with men? How can we still experience the presence of the Lord as the great Guest and Host at our family meals? And sacramentally at the Lord's supper?

3. How was Sarah's laughter upon hearing God's promise of a son (p. 117) different from Abraham's earlier laughter upon receiving this good news?

4. In his prayer of intercession for Sodom, how did Abraham express his calling as co-worker with God in the covenant?

5. How was Abraham to become God's fellow worker in the covenant with respect to his descendants?

6. In his prayer Abraham appeals to the righteousness of God. Why such an appeal? Is righteousness central in the Biblical witness about God in His relationship to the world? How was God's righteousness fully revealed in Jesus Christ? In what way does Abraham's prayer foreshadow the mediatorial work of Christ?

7. Do believers and unbelievers suffer together under God's judgments upon the earth? Is there also an important dimension of difference in the way they suffer?

8. How do both boldness and reverence come to balanced expression in Abraham's prayer?

# 14: The Judge of All the Earth

*Genesis 19*

1. Abraham prayed, "Shall not the Judge of all the earth do right?" God's response was the destruction of Sodom. How did God demonstrate His righteous judgment against Sodom? What evidence do we have that Sodom was ripe for such destruction? What was God's final test?

2. Explain De Graaf's statement that "God judges people according to their ties with Him" (p. 120). Were Lot's ties with God different from those of the other inhabitants of Sodom? In what way? By what means does God maintain His claim upon people, even those without a knowledge of His special revelation? (Rom. 1:18-25; Acts 13:13ff; 14:8-18; 17:22-33). Can we say that God judges people according to the light of revelation that they have received? Does more light mean heavier judgment upon disobedience, and less light means lighter judgment? How do the words of Christ in Matthew 10:12-15 and 11:20-24 shed light on this question of the urgent need for repentance? What is now our responsibility in the light of the fullness of God's revelation in Jesus Christ?

3. What comparison does Christ draw between the judgment upon Sodom and the judgment which will accompany His second coming? (Luke 17:28-30).

4. How does Sodom serve as a symbol of "the great city" where anti-Christian powers lash out against the servants of the Lord? (Rev. 11:1-14).

5. Can we ever hope to fully understand God's ways in bringing His righteous judgments upon the earth, touching the lives of both believers and unbelievers?

6. Where did Lot stand in the midst of Sodom's downfall? Did he take a clear-cut position? Did he compromise? Did he witness against the evils of the city? Was he also drawn into their wicked life-style? Was he a believer at heart? A strong believer? A weak one? (See II Peter 2:7-8).

7. What does it mean that God in His righteous judgment rained destruction upon Sodom for His own name's sake and for the sake of the covenant He made with Abraham, looking ahead to its fulfillment in the coming Christ? Did Lot and his descendants end up on the side of the covenant people or on the other side?

# 15: The Protection of the Promised Seed

*Genesis 20*

1. Why is it important in this Bible story to put the central emphasis on God's protecting care rather than on the weakness of Abraham's faith? What happens when we reverse this order? How does this question touch on the very core of the Biblical message? Is the Bible a revelation of the mighty acts of God in the salvation of His people or a record of human obedient and disobedient responses to God's Word? Which is primary and which secondary?

2. Is there any way we can enter understandingly into this almost unbelievable collapse of faith on the part of Abraham and Sarah? Their unbelief seems to have arisen from fear. What fear? And in the face of what sure promise that God had given them shortly before?

3. What was really at stake in this sorry affair? Abraham's life? Sarah's chastity? Their marriage? Their promised son? Or was all of this wrapped up in the covenant promise of God which pointed toward the salvation of His people and His world in the coming Messiah? What was God protecting when He rescued Abraham and Sarah from their own foolish scheme?

4. Were there historical reasons for Abraham and Sarah to fear violence at the hands of people like the Canaanites and Philistines, and especially their rulers?

5. What must we think when a believer like Abraham is rebuked for his sins by an unbeliever? Was Abraham overwhelmed by

shame? Did he confess his guilt? Did he witness to God's grace? Or did he frame excuses and try to give grounds for his fear? How are we to evaluate Abraham's betrayal of God's blessing? Was Peter's later betrayal of Christ in some ways similar to that of Abraham? Does God's work of salvation rest upon His faithfulness or ours?

6. Abimelech here proclaims the gospel to Abraham. Do unbelievers sometimes stand closer to the truth than believers? Do we, like Abraham and Peter, sometimes get ourselves into situations where we act out of fear rather than faith, looking for ways to cover up our sins instead of living the truth?

7. Looking at God's past promises, his present life, and the future hope of salvation, what was Abraham really rejecting in the "white lie" he told to Abimelech?

8. How does this episode make it clear that the victory of faith and the power for obedient living lies *outside* ourselves in the saving work of God through His promised Messiah? How is this realization related to Paul's testimony that "we are more than conquerors through Him who loved us"? (Rom. 8:37). Does God often have to work out His plan *despite* His people? Does God's Word ever fail?

9. Is it God's judgment or His forgiving grace and mercy that finally leads believers to repentance and renewed obedience?

# 16: Divine Good Pleasure

*Genesis 21*

1. There is a note of surprise running through Bible history—God coming through with surprising events, evoking laughter of amazement among His people. How was this true in the birth of Isaac ("laughter")? Was this also true in the birth of Christ?

2. Earlier it was clear that God was working out His covenant purposes through Abraham alone, not Abraham *and* Lot. Now He was working through Isaac alone, not Isaac *and* Ishmael. Is

this also true of Christ? Is our salvation in "Christ alone" (as Luther and Calvin put it), rather than in some pattern of cooperation between Christ *and* us?

3. What was Isaac's special role in the unfolding plan of covenant history?

4. Is Ishmael's jealousy understandable? Was his struggle also our struggle? Was it the struggle to recognize that the key to salvation lies outside ourselves in Christ Jesus, rather than in our own independence and importance? Is such self-denial easy?

5. What are the tragic consequences of drifting away from the covenant community, as Hagar and Ishmael did?

6. In later Bible history, Ishmael and Isaac and their descendants came into contact with each other from time to time (see Gen. 25:7-18). Is such contact with the covenant people important for those who stand outside the inner circle of God's plan of salvation? Did Ishmael and his descendants benefit from this contact?

7. What blessing did God bestow upon the house of Ishmael? What does this tell us about God's relationship to other peoples, those outside of Israel? Did God completely forget about them? What does it mean that God's promise to Abraham and his descendants was to be a source of blessing to all peoples? Does the concentration of God's saving work in Israel exclude all concern with other nations? Explain the statement by De Graaf that one day in Christ God would reach out with His saving grace to all nations (p. 132). Was God's particular concern with Abraham, Isaac, Jacob, and the Israelites an *end* in itself or a *means* to a larger end, namely, His universal offer of salvation to the whole world? Is it true that God set out to redeem the world, and that His promise to the ancient patriarchs was the beginning of that cosmic plan of salvation?

8. How important are earthly covenants and business contracts, such as the one between Abraham and Abimelech? How are all such human covenants to be honored in the light of the all-embracing covenant which God makes with believers?

# 17:  On the Mount of the Lord

*Genesis 22*

1. What is there about this Bible story that makes it so centrally important for understanding the ongoing message of Scripture as a whole?

2. In speaking to Abraham, God referred to Isaac as "your son, your only son, whom you love." Do these words remind you of the words the New Testament uses in speaking about Christ as "God's only begotten Son" and His "beloved Son"?

3. Why did the very idea of human sacrifice make Abraham's trial of faith the more intense? What was the meaning of animal sacrifice in Old Testament times? (Think of Abel, Noah, Abraham himself, and the later priests of Israel.) In the fullness of the times, God made the sacrifice of the Man, Jesus Christ. Could we ever understand that sacrifice without the Old Testament?

4. How does the sacrifice of Isaac point forward to the sacrifice of Christ? How were these two sacrifices similar? How were they different?

5. This event was a test of Abraham's faith. But even more, it was a test of God's faithfulness to His covenant promises. How was God being tested?

6. In what sense was Abraham's sacrifice an imitation of God's greater sacrifice?

7. What do you think Abraham had in mind when he answered Isaac's stunning question by saying, "God will provide himself the lamb for a burnt offering"?

8. What gave Abraham the courage to go through with this severe test of trust in God's promise? (Heb. 11:18-19).

9. What is the forward-looking importance of the name given to this mountain, namely, *Moriah*?

10. How does the Bible's central teaching concerning substitutionary atonement come to expression prophetically here at Mount Moriah?  How does it later come to climactic expression at

Golgotha?

11. How was Abraham himself blessed through this sacrifice of Isaac by looking ahead to the sacrifice of his coming Child, Jesus Christ? What did Christ mean in saying, "Father Abraham rejoiced to see my day; he saw it and was glad"? (John 8:56-9).

12. What is the relationship between God's great sacrifice in Christ and the sacrifices to which He calls us? In what sense do the sufferings of God's people for righteousness' sake involve a sacrifice by God for us? Is it too much that God expects of us a complete sacrifice of our lives in His service? Can we make such sacrifices in our own strength? Or are we only giving back to God what He has first given us?

# 18:  The Guarantee of the Inheritance

*Genesis 23*

1. In the light of this passage and the total witness of the Scriptures, how should believers view their own death and the death of their dear ones?

2. What is the meaning of De Graaf's statement that "from beginning to end, Scripture is a book of this earth"? (p. 142).

3. What place does mourning at the time of death have in the life of a believer?

4. Is the grave the end of everything?

5. Burial is a symbol of hope in our final glorification. Does it also symbolize hope in the final glorification of the earth in which we are buried?

6. What strength and comfort can we derive from knowing that Christ has gone before us into death and risen again to newness of life?

7. Why was it important that Sarah and later Abraham himself and the other patriarchs were buried within the land of promise? In what sense were these burials a guarantee of the promised inheritance of the land of Canaan? How did the burial of Sarah

reflect Abraham's confidence in the sure fulfillment of the covenant?

8. Why did Abraham insist upon a separate burial place for Sarah which he could call his own, rather than burying her in a grave borrowed from the Hittites?

9. Why did Abraham insist on buying it, rather than accepting it as a gift from the Hittites?

10. How is Jesus Christ the fulfillment of everything which this event stands for?


# 19:  Loving God for His Own Sake

*Job 1*

1. Sketch the background and setting of the book of Job. Who was this man Job? Where did he live? Are there any known connections between Job and Abraham? How is it possible that this "outsider" knew about God and served Him? Describe his family life. Who wrote this dramatic story?

2. This book of Job wrestles with the problem of suffering. Why is there suffering in the world? What is the purpose of suffering in the life of believers, such as Job? Is their suffering more intense than that of other men? Why?

3. How are we to understand De Graaf's statements that Job's love of God is rooted in Jesus Christ (p. 149), seeing that Christ was not to appear until centuries later?

4. What task has God assigned to angels? Why are they called "ministering spirits"? (Heb. 1:14).

5. What role does satan and his evil host play in world history? How does his wicked purpose come to expression in the book of Job? What criticism did he bring against Job and, indirectly, against God Himself? Were there grounds for this criticism in Job's life? In our lives?

6. What was God's evaluation of Job's life? How is it possible that

His was so radically different from satan's? Was Job, then, a perfect, sinless man? What was the strength of his life?

7. What did it mean for Job to love God for His own sake? What does it mean for us? Does it mean wanting *God Himself*, not just the things He gives? Does it mean clinging to God, regardless of what He gives or fails to give us? If we love God simply because He is God, can we still trust Him even when everything seems to go wrong? Is that what we find in Job? Are there earthly analogies to such love of God? Do people love fathers or mothers or marriage partners simply for who they are, apart from any consideration of personal benefit? How does such pure love come to perfect expression in Jesus Christ?

8. What series of hostile actions did satan take against Job? Was he testing God as well as Job? Does satan have unlimited powers? Can we fully understand how a good God can allow such demonic powers to be set loose upon men? What is the meaning of Christ's words "I saw Satan fall like lightning from heaven"? (Luke 10:18). Why did Christ say, "If it is by the finger of God that I cast out demons, then the kingdom of God has come upon you"? (Luke 11:20). What does it mean that God has bound satan for a thousand years? (Rev. 20:2).

9. How did Job react to all his adversities? Did he stand or fall? Where did he find strength—in himself or in the God he loved? How did he confess this amid the awful calamities which befell him?

## 20: The Lord's Involvement in Human Suffering

*Job 2-39*

1. Do you suppose Job could have coined the phrase "Lord, save me from my friends"? Or "With friends like that, who needs enemies?" Why were Job's friends such miserable comforters?

2. What was their "logical explanation" for Job's troubles? Did Jesus' disciples also share this view of the relationship between

sin and suffering? (John 9:2). May we ever draw the conclusion that those who suffer most must be the greatest sinners? (Luke 13:1-5). Is suffering traceable to specific sins? Or is it the result of the burden of guilt that we bear with all men corporately because of our universal sinfulness?

3. How did Job waver between confessing and denying God's justice, righteousness and fairness?

4. In our suffering, as in Job's, how can God be *for* us and *against* us at the same time? Why is an understanding of God's covenant relationship with His people crucial in seeking to understand this twofold attitude of God toward us in our suffering? Did the fact that Job stood outside the inner circle of God's covenant with Abraham make it more difficult for him to understand God's ways? What does it mean that in His covenant God has bound Himself to man and His whole creation, come what may?

5. Explain De Graaf's statement that even though Job was a believer, he still placed himself at the center of this drama, rather than keeping God central (p. 155). How did this add to his troubles?

6. Is it really possible, by faith, to accept personal suffering and the sufferings of the world so completely as coming from God's hand and as being under His control that we can endure them as means of sanctification? Do we really believe that God sanctifies us and the world through suffering?

7. What is the meaning of De Graaf's statement that "the world will forever bear the mark of the cross"? (p. 155). Does this refer to the crosses we bear or to the cross of Christ? What does the cross symbolize?

8. How was God involved in Job's suffering? How is He involved in ours? And centrally in the sufferings of Jesus Christ?

9. How was the suffering of Job different from that of his wife? Does this difference still hold today between believers and unbelievers?

10. People sometimes speak of "the patience of Job." Was Job really so patient? Or did he become desperately impatient?

11. Was Job a victim of misfortune? Or a child being chastised by his Father? Or a "test case" to prove a point to satan? Or an example of persevering faith? Or should the emphasis fall upon the preserving grace of God? The Hand that allowed the suffering was also the Hand that sustained Job's life.

12. Can you find evidence that in the depths of his suffering Job was crying out for a mediator, one to stand between him and God to judge his cause? (See Job 9:33 in context). How were Job's pleadings finally answered in the sufferings of Christ? Why was Christ the only One perfectly able to keep on holding fast to God even in the depths of indescribable misery?

13. Though the words of the three friends did more harm than good, God's Word finally set the record straight, putting Job in his place and giving him a new lease on life. What did God say? (See Job 38-39).

# 21: Sanctification unto Renewal

*Job 40-42*

1. In the light of Scripture, De Graaf divides all world history into three main periods, which also form the three motifs of all Biblical revelation, namely, creation, fall, and redemption. Does this division do justice to the givens of Scripture and history? How is this division reflected in the life history of Job as told dramatically in this book that bears his name?

2. Why is it important to emphasize that God's saving grace leads to the restoration of earthly life for Job and for all believers? Do we tend to push salvation off "beyond the blue horizon" into "the sweet bye and bye"? Reflect on this central thesis: redemption in Christ is the restoration of a fallen creation.

3. Do we now see such restoration as already fully realized? When will it be ours in perfection? In the meantime, how should we wait for it patiently? Is the apparent delay of the new earth under new heavens a trial of faith? Do we await it eagerly? Should we also work for the final coming of the Kingdom of God? How?

How did Job go about renewing his family life and his work?

4. What can we learn from seeing Job praying for his three friends? Why did God order him to do so? In what sense had they not spoken rightly about God and Job? What does it mean that they were man-centered instead of God-centered?

5. Job, as mediator, intercedes for his friends. How does his prayer point forward to the mediating and interceding work of Jesus Christ? What is the fundamental difference between Job's prayer and Christ's? Did Job have to pray for his own forgiveness too? Did Christ? If Christ prayed for others, should we also pray for our fellow men and for the needs of the world? What should enter into those prayers?

6. How did God finally humble Job and bring him back to childlike submission to His will? Why is it important to learn the lesson of listening in silence to the voice of God's majesty and love?

7. Even though God restored Job to a new life, Job had to walk in the shadow of the cross the rest of his days. What cross did he have to bear?

8. The restoration which came in the end was a victory for both God and Job. Explain this. What does this suggest about the interrelation of God's acts and our acts in all of life?


# 22: The Preservation of the Covenant Seed

*Genesis 24—25:18*

1. After an interlude of three chapters dealing with Job, we return now to God's way in the lives of the patriarchs. Be sure you can recall clearly the leading actors in this covenant drama of redemption—Abraham, his wife Sarah, and their two sons Ishmael and Isaac. Now comes the quest for a wife for Isaac, which leads to Rebekah.

2. Explain the two dangers that constantly threatened the life of Abraham and his descendants, i.e. mingling with the Canaanites

and returning to Haran, their former homeland. Were these dangers real? How did Abraham's life situation in Canaan make these possibilities a real temptation? Did the descendants of Abraham (the Israelites) later fall into similar temptations— wanting to return to Egypt and intermarrying with the unbelieving peoples around them?

3. What was at stake in God's desire that Abraham lead a separate life and be different from the people around him? Was it merely Abraham's spiritual well-being? Or the preservation of the covenant line? Did it have anything to do with the coming of the promised Messiah?

4. Are we also called to live separate lives? Is spiritual separation an end in itself, or a means to a larger end? What end? What happens when we lose sight of the call to spiritual separation and dedication to the Lord? Does this call mean living apart from the unbelieving society around us, in separate communities, or does it mean maintaining our religious distinctiveness while being involved in the life of the world?

5. How did Abraham and his servant, Eliezar, express their confidence that God would honor their holy intentions in safeguarding the covenant seed? What sign did the servant look for when he arrived in Haran? Why did such signs play an important role on the way toward the coming Christ?

6. What was involved in Rebekah's weighty decision to break with her father's house and homeland? Whose call was she answering? How does her choice speak to us? Can we learn anything from it as we examine our own readiness to submit to the will of God for our lives?

7. The marriage of Isaac and Rebekah was rooted in the belief that God had brought them together. By what means can we express a similar faith in our marriages and other life relationships?

8. How does it become clear that God was concentrating His covenant promise specifically in Isaac and his descendants? What spiritual choice did Ishmael and his descendants make?

9. Why did Abraham command that he be buried in the grave he had purchased for Sarah? Why in the land of Canaan rather than some other area, such as Ur of the Chaldeans, the land of

his fathers? Even in death, Abraham was declaring his faith in the covenant promise of God. How was his burial a sign of the inheritance? How did this sign point forward in hope toward the coming Christ?

## 23: Flesh and Spirit

*Genesis 25:19-34*

1. Here the accent falls on the sharp religious contrast between Jacob and Esau, which De Graaf describes as the antithesis between "spirit" and "flesh." How are these two Biblical concepts, "flesh" and "spirit," to be understood? Do they represent a conflict between the body ("flesh") as evil and the soul ("spirit") as good? Is this true to the Bible's way of speaking about such things? Was Esau's way of life based upon the body and Jacob's upon the soul? Or are "flesh" and "spirit" Biblical symbols pointing respectively to the principle of unbelief and the principle of belief, which are at enmity with each other? See Romans 8:5-7. See also Romans 12:1-2, where Paul appeals to us to dedicate ourselves, body and soul, to the service of God.

2. The clash between Esau and Jacob is a further expression of the great conflict that goes back to the very dawn of human history. Can you trace it back to the two hostile "seeds" of Genesis 3? How was it also present in Abraham's household? In what form did Christ face it during His earthly ministry? Is it still with us today? How do we experience it in our world?

3. Isn't it disturbing to see such bitter conflict arising in a covenant home such as the home of Isaac and Rebekah? Did these parents themselves contribute to the conflict through their partiality, Isaac siding with Esau and Rebekah with Jacob? Where did they first go wrong?

4. God's electing love was at work in the decision that the older and stronger brother should be by-passed in favor of the younger and weaker. Was this choice based upon any merit on Jacob's part? Was he better and holier than his brother Esau? Does the fact

that God so often chooses the weak and foolish, as in this case, tell us something about His method and purpose in working out His plan of salvation? (see I Cor. 1:26-31).

5. Is divine election at odds with our human responsibility to repent and believe and obey?

6. How would you describe the sharp differences in personality between Jacob and Esau? Was it the difference between a "good guy" and a "bad guy"? Or were they both unworthy of the covenant blessing? Yet, how are we to understand the Biblical teaching that, despite everything, Jacob was at bottom a man of faith and Esau a man of unbelief? How can saving faith and very questionable deeds go hand in hand as in the life of Jacob?

7. What was the spiritual importance of the birthright blessing within the line of the covenant?

8. Both Jacob and Esau misunderstood the spirit and meaning of the birthright blessing. Show how Esau misunderstood it by failing to sense its *value*, and Jacob by failing to sense its *wonder* as a gift of God's grace.

9. Explain how God's judgments descended on all the members of this covenant family because of their distorted responses to the covenant promise. Jacob had to flee the home life he loved so much. Esau was swindled out of his inheritance. Rebekah had to part with her favorite son. Isaac became a broken man. Work out these ideas on the basis of the passage at hand.

10. Does God elect people unto a personal privileged status? (Think of Jacob, who wanted to use God's favor for self-advancement.) Or is election unto service of God and fellow men? See Acts 9:15; Ephesians 1:4; 2:10; I Peter 2:9.

11. Does the Biblical teaching concerning God's election make our choices and decisions meaningless? In view of the radical antithesis between faith and unbelief, as expressed in this and other parts of the Bible, how important is it that we take the right side in making our decision?

# 24: Rehoboth

*Genesis 26*

1. God's people in the land of Canaan repeatedly found themselves under heavy pressure from the two great power centers of the day—Mesopotamia in the east and Egypt to the west. Originally the patriarchs had come out of Mesopotamia, and later their descendants would return there as captives of Babylon. Egypt, on the other hand, became Israel's house of of bondage. Again and again, God's people sought refuge there in times of famine. In the passage at hand, Isaac is headed for Egypt. But the Lord stops him in Gerar, still part of the land of promise, and commands him to stay there rather than go on to Egypt. In view of the covenant inheritance, why was it important that Isaac remain in the promised land?

2. Isaac was a passive person—not a pioneering type like his father Abraham or his son Jacob. He seems to have done little more than imitate Abraham, going to the same places (Gerar), digging the same wells, giving them the same names—simply walking in his father's footsteps. He even repeated his father's lies about his wife being his sister. What does this tell us about Isaac's role in the historical development of the covenant line? Did he do much more than maintain the *status quo*? Was he just a link between Abraham and Jacob?

3. How did Isaac's weakness endanger the promised inheritance of the land?

4. How did his spirit of backing off from his rightful possessions threaten the future hope of the coming Christ?

5. Was Isaac moved by a deep and strong awareness of his identity and calling within the covenant? What was at stake—his own personal rights, or the covenant rights of his heirs from whom would come the Messiah?

6. Why did Isaac name the third well, which was not disputed, *Rehoboth*? What does this name mean? Why was "room" in the land always a thorny, critical problem for the patriarchs? What was at issue in the struggle for "room"?

7. Why did God protect the marriage of Isaac and Rebekah? What was ultimately at stake?

8. Like Abraham, Isaac makes a covenant at Beersheba with the ruler of Gerar. In what sense does this indicate a turn for the better in Isaac's life? How does this reflect growing strength and independence in Isaac's conduct? What covenantal significance should we attach to Abimelech's official recognition of Isaac as a prince in the land?

# 25: God's Prerogative in Election

*Genesis 27—28:9*

1. God adopts some very questionable children into His covenant family. Look at the tangled mess these four people made of their family life. Show how the blame for this very unholy situation was shared by Isaac, Rebekah, Esau, and Jacob alike. How did it happen that the Rebekah-Jacob coalition began plotting against the Isaac-Esau alliance?

2. But there is also a fifth Actor in this drama, who is really its Director. God intervenes to overrule these sinful schemes. What is this divine perspective which De Graaf says we must take? How does God preserve His covenant promise and His purpose according to election? Can God bend sinful human motives to accomplish His goals?

3. How did Esau demonstrate his rejection of the covenant, even though he still wanted its earthly blessing? How did his mixed marriages endanger the life of the chosen people and the promise of the coming Savior? Is the choice of a marriage partner still a crucial faith decision in our times?

4. What benefits would have come to Esau if he had been content to share in Jacob's special blessing, rather than trying to seize the prize by bribing his father without actually intending to break with his worldly ways?

5. How did the friction between Esau and Jacob show up later in

the hostilities between Edom and Israel? Who won these battles? Or did both sides become losers? Were there also winners on both sides—those who accepted the Christ? In the massacre at Bethlehem (Matt. 2) we see Herod, a son of Esau, an Edomite ruler over Israel, striking out at the chosen Son of Jacob, the Christ Child. Can this brutal act of murderous hatred be traced back to the sharp clash within Isaac's household?

6. How can we explain Isaac's insistence on favoring Esau in spite of God's clear choice of Jacob, so that he wound up blessing Jacob against his will? Was he ignorant of God's will? Or, did he know it and refuse to submit to it? What evidence is there that he finally accepted God's choice of Jacob?

7. Explain De Graaf's statement: "It's amazing how faith and sin were mixed together in Rebekah" (p. 189). How did her *faith* in God's prophetic Word concerning her two sons come to expression? What was the basic *sin* in her actions? What if she had argued that the end justifies the means?

8. Why was it important for Jacob to leave home and seek a wife among distant relatives? Was Rebekah's argument for such action beyond reproach? What were the dangers of mixed marriage confronting Jacob in Canaan? What was ultimately at stake in his selection of a wife? Does Isaac's approval suggest that he, too, was now willing to face the truth regarding Esau and submit to God's will for Jacob?

# 26: God's Primacy in the Covenant

*Genesis 28:10-22*

1. Can we reconstruct Jacob's spiritual state of mind as he left home? Were his real reasons for fleeing and his stated reason the same? Was his desire for the covenant blessing rightly motivated? Did he enjoy a close walk with the Lord? Who seems to have been first in his life—God or Jacob?

2. How serious was it that Jacob was being cast out of the covenant circle? Was that a judgment? Or a blessing? Or was God blen-

ding judgment and blessing together in working out His plan of salvation?

3. How does this Bethel event reveal God's primacy and initiative in the covenant? Did God wait until Jacob was "good enough" before entering into this personal relationship with him? Or did God take Jacob as he was in order eventually (at Peniel) to make him into what he ought to be? Does the covenant rest at bottom on Jacob's faithfulness, and ours, or upon the faithfulness of God? Is the covenant based upon *our* inner attitudes, and Jacob's, or upon God's decision for the world in Jesus Christ?

4. What is the significance of that place called *Bethel*? What does the name itself mean? Why did Jacob give it that name? What role did Bethel play in Jacob's later life (see Gen. 35:1-15) and in the ongoing history of Israel? (see I Kings 12:25-33). In what sense can we say that the whole world has become our "Bethel" now that Christ has come and the Holy Spirit has been poured out? Do we still need such "holy places" today? Does Bethel also point forward to our worship and service of God on the new earth? How does the entire history of Bethel indicate once again that our faith should lead us to live in a down-to-earth way?

5. What meaning should we attach to the fact that God revealed Himself to Jacob in a dream concerning a *ladder*, a stairway? Whom do we see at the top of the ladder? Who is at the bottom? What is the importance of the angels ascending and descending? How does this scene reveal a new personal relationship of communion and fellowship which God was there establishing with Jacob? How does Christ later apply this dream to Himself? (John 1:43ff, especially vs. 51).

6. What is the importance of Jacob's act of anointing with oil the stone that had served as his pillow? Could this act be construed as a pagan way of worshiping? What did Jacob mean by it? How are we to understand the vow he made? Does this vow seem to reflect his personal acceptance of the covenant promises made to Abraham? Can we say that Jacob was converted overnight? Or was it a long process? Did he eventually live up to this vow?

# 27: The Word Becomes Flesh

*Genesis 29-30*

1. Does the title of this chapter make you think ahead to the New Testament? (John 1:14). How did the Word of promise, spoken repeatedly throughout the Old Testament, come to its fulfillment, taking on flesh and blood in Jesus Christ?

2. How did these forward-looking promises of God's Word take on further shape in Jacob's life? How were they being realized with respect to his children, possessions and land? Were they also gradually emerging in Jacob's personality? How was God at work breaking down his old nature and building up his new nature? Did Jacob learn the lessons of sanctification quickly and easily? Did he have to pay the price for his slowness to repent and believe and obey?

3. In Uncle Laban, the deceiver Jacob finally met his match. Point out how their dealings with each other were marked again and again by trickery and deception.

4. How was God's Word of promise constantly at work in all the greediness and schemings of these rivals, so that His covenant plan could triumph?

5. In the light of Scripture, how should we view Jacob's polygamy? Did God tolerate polygamy in Old Testament times? Was it part of His original creation order? How does the New Testament move believers gradually toward a one-to-one marriage relationship?

6. What family troubles did Jacob experience because of his unhealthy marriage relationships? Did God use even these strained relationships to push forward the unfolding history of His covenant people?

7. What important role did Jacob's twelve sons play in later Old Testament history? Do the twelve sons have anything to do with Christ's appointment of twelve apostles? What special Messianic prophecy was attached to Jacob's son Judah? Did this prophecy also come to fulfillment in the New Testament?

8. What was wrong with settling down in Haran? How did God see

to it that Jacob would not feel at home there? What was the importance of Jacob's intended return to the land of promise?

9. Were Jacob's manifold blessings the result of his clever dealings? Or did they come to him in spite of his devious ways? Did God bestow them for His own good reasons—His faithfulness to the covenant promise, His commitment to the coming Messiah?

# 28: Separation by the Word

*Genesis 31*

1. In the title of this chapter, how are we to understand De Graaf's emphasis on "the Word"? What was the message of that Word? How was that message revealed to Jacob? What historical factors were involved in this separation brought about by the Word of God?

2. After about twenty years in Haran, was it possible for Jacob's family to make a complete break with the spirit of Haran? How did the influence of Haran show up in Jacob's family life, just as the influence of the surrounding Canaanites showed up later in the life of his descendants?

3. In the light of studies by modern archeology, are we now able to give a better interpretation of Rachel's secret act of carrying off her father's "idols"? Was her deed a violation of the second commandment (idolatry), or was it rather a violation of the eighth commandment (stealing)? Could it be that these "teraphim" served as deeds to personal property? Check a contemporary book on archeology.

4. Should we view the working relationships between Laban and Jacob as a model for employer-employee relationships today? Does the Bible offer norms for this sphere of activity in our lives?

5. What were the immediate causes of the growing estrangement between the families of Laban and Jacob? Were there also

deeper causes related to the fulfillment of the covenant promise?

6. The central point is that God was keeping watch over His unworthy covenant heir even in this foreign country. Was God's electing love based on Jacob's merits? Did Jacob deserve the rich blessings that came to him as heir to the covenant promise? Or was his salvation, too, by grace alone? Show how God's hand was present working through all the unholy strivings in the life of Laban and Jacob.

7. How did the settlement finally reached by Laban and Jacob reflect Laban's recognition of Jacob as a man in his own right and the recipient of God's covenant blessing?

8. Look at Laban's words in Genesis 31:49: "The LORD watch between you and me, when we are absent one from the other." Often these words are spoken as a parting blessing among believers. But was this really a blessing? Or was it a solemn warning between these two men? Since neither one trusted the other, were they calling on God to keep the peace between them when they turned their backs upon each other?

9. What was the nature of the covenant between Jacob and Laban? What was the agreement they reached? Did past experience teach them that some sort of assurance was needed to keep them from rising up in anger against each other? How did the pile of stones serve as a witness to their covenant? Was a marker drawing the borderline between them necessary? How did this "earthly covenant" contribute to the unfolding of the special covenant of grace which God had made with Abraham, Isaac, and now Jacob?

# 29: Israel's God

*Genesis 32-33*

1. De Graaf says that until now, God was willing to "overlook" Jacob's sins (p. 210). How are we to understand this? Did God simply close His eyes to those sins? Just push them aside? Put up

with them? Or was God storing them up in memory, awaiting the right moment to refine and renew Jacob?

2. For Jacob, going home meant facing his estranged brother Esau. Why did Jacob have reason to fear this meeting? After years of separation, what seems to have been Esau's attitude toward Jacob as they approached each other? Was Jacob's spirit now different than it had been years before? Was he less self-reliant? Less deceitful? More submissive to God's will? More ready to confess his sins?

3. In wrestling with that Man at Peniel, feelings of both fear and hope arose in Jacob's heart. What was the cause of his fears? On what did he pin his hopes? How do Jacob's words, pressed out of him during this struggle in the darkness, reflect a change in his life—a change from dependence on the "flesh" to dependence upon the "spirit"?

4. What does it mean that "God had chosen Jacob as His opponent"? (p. 213). Explain the clear Scriptural emphasis that Jacob's strength in this encounter lay in his tenacious clinging to God's covenant promises.

5. What is the meaning of the Peniel encounter? Was this the real turning point in Jacob's life? How is this reflected in the way God changed his name from *Jacob* to *Israel*? Are there parallels between Jacob's Peniel experience and the Damascus Road experience in Paul's life? (Acts 9:1-9). Should every Christian have a Peniel or a Damascus Road experience?

6. How does Jacob's struggle at Peniel point forward to the struggles of Christ in Gethsemane and at Golgotha? What similarities can we see? What radical difference? Whose sins lay at the bottom of Jacob's wrestlings—and Christ's? How was Christ's encounter with God the fulfillment of Jacob's?

7. How can we account for Jacob's victory? Did the old, conniving Jacob succeed in outsmarting even God? Did he outlast God in this endurance contest? Or did the secret of Jacob's strength lie in the strength of his opponent? Did God allow Himself to be overcome? Did He let Jacob win? In what sense was Jacob's victory the result of standing on the promises of God and pleading God's mercy? Is it true, even today, that God "allows Himself to be overcome by our prayers"? (p. 215).

8. One of the lasting results of Peniel was Jacob's limp. What did this limp remind him of constantly? Another result was the courage Jacob found, a courage that enabled him to meet his brother Esau without his old fears. Why was this now possible?

9. At long last God had prepared his stubborn servant Jacob to return to Canaan. How was this the fulfillment of God's covenant promise? And also of the promise which Jacob himself had made some twenty years before at Bethel? (Gen. 28:18-22). May we conclude that God's purpose was not to allow Jacob to live in that dedicated land of promise until he himself had become a dedicated man of God?

# 30: Holy is the Lord

*Genesis 34-36*

1. What reasons can be given for Jacob's rather lengthy delay-in-route at Shechem? How does Jacob's delay in returning to Bethel reflect his slowness in keeping his promise and his weak, inadequate understanding of the covenantal calling to live a life of holiness before the Lord?

2. Aren't you amazed at the patience of God in putting up with the failures of Jacob again and again, almost without end? At Jacob's slowness in coming to a new life-style? At God's faithfulness to His covenant in spite of Jacob's repeated unfaithfulness?

3. What dangers did Jacob bring upon his family by continuing to live in Shechem? When calamity finally struck Dinah, was the outrage of her brothers justifiable? Were they concerned about preserving the purity of the covenant family? Was their zeal admirable? Can we approve of their means in attempting to set right the wrong which had taken place? How was their evil plan an attack on the very sign and seal of the covenant? How did God use even this sinful situation to separate Jacob and his family from the pagan relationships that threatened to destroy them?

4. How did the danger of worldly entanglements continue to plague the future life of the covenant people in Canaan? Were they strong enough to stand on their own feet? How did God remedy this situation via a temporary—but lengthy—stay in Egypt?

5. What was the importance of the fact that Jacob finally did return to Bethel? What if he had gone willingly and immediately— instead of waiting until God's judgments pushed him in that direction? What preparations were necessary before Jacob could in good conscience meet God at Bethel? How did this meeting help bring Jacob to greater single-heartedness in serving the Lord?

6. What was the significance of Jacob's act of rejecting the name *Benoni* for his twelfth son in favor of *Benjamin*?

7. What happened at that final family reunion? How was that empty chair for mother Rebekah a judgment upon the earlier evil scheme of Rebekah and Jacob? (Gen. 27:41-5). Why was it important for Jacob's entire household to receive the covenant blessing from old father Isaac? How did this separation of Jacob and Esau set the stage for later conflicts between their descendants?

# 31: Sold for Twenty Pieces of Silver

*Genesis 37-38*

1. Does it disturb you to see how God's covenant people again and again fall deeply into sinful practices? Would you think more highly of the Bible if it had passed these failures by in silence? What does such honesty tell us about the kind of book the Bible is? Does its emphasis fall upon man's worthiness or God's faithfulness? Could Jacob's family have survived and would the Messiah have come apart from God's hand in the history of salvation?

2. Explain the point that De Graaf makes concerning the forward-looking thrust of these patriarchal stories (p. 223). Why was the writer of Genesis in such a hurry?

3. The tensions and conflicts which were present in the families of Abraham and Isaac seem to repeat themselves in Jacob's family. What was the source of strife between the children of Leah and Rachel? Was the continuation of the covenant dependent on the exemplary conduct of Jacob's sons or on God's keeping His promise to Abraham?

4. Were the troubles that arose due largely to the failure of Jacob's family to lead a life apart? Were Jacob's sons too open to the evil influences of the surrounding Canaanite peoples? How did this show up?

5. In Joseph's life, how was divine revelation mixed with personal pride? How was a true sense of righteousness mixed with a spirit of arrogance? Was he right in bringing father Jacob reports about his brothers' evil deeds?

6. How are we to understand the rising prominence of Judah among Jacob's sons? How are both shame and honor revealed in Judah's life? Was God's choice of Judah as the special ancestor of Christ based on personal merit or amazing grace?

7. Was the brothers' hatred of Joseph rooted in Jacob's favoritism? Or Joseph's dreams? Or did it also grow out of Joseph's witness to the truth?

8. When Joseph's brothers sold him as a slave, were they following general practices of that day? What must we think of slavery in the light of Scripture? (Note also the New Testament epistle, Philemon.) Was selling Joseph into slavery more compassionate than killing him or letting him die in the pit? Were the brothers trying to get rid of God's witness to the truth among them? Was their act merely the result of bad relationships? Or did it also reflect a lack of covenant consciousness?

9. If the brothers' evil plot had succeeded, how would this have led to the destruction of the covenant line? How was God's hand at work in this awful bargain? What was God's intention?

10. In what ways was Joseph a symbol of the coming Christ?

11. Reuben was disqualified, Judah was dishonored, and Joseph was gone. What did the future of the covenant promise now depend on? Was there any human way out? Or would Jacob's family have to await the surprising and mysterious leading of God?

# 32:  God's Word in Egypt

*Genesis 39-41*

1. Joseph now represents God's Word in Egypt. Christ is also called God's Word (John 1:14). How does Joseph pre-figure the coming Christ? What is the difference between the Word of God *coming* to and through Joseph in Egypt and Christ *being* the Word of God incarnate for the world?

2. Dreams play an important role in these Joseph stories. Did dreams have a special significance for the Egyptians? Did God also use them as means of revelation? Is it strange that these dream-revelations should be given even to unbelievers? How do you suppose God revealed the meaning of these dreams to Joseph?

3. Why is it important to emphasize Joseph's office and calling to serve as God's representative and witness in Egypt—rather than his personal virtues and exemplary character?

4. How did Joseph's witness to God's Word come to expression in Potiphar's home? Did Potiphar's wife, by reason of her superior position, have the right to lay claim to sexual relations with Joseph? What trust would Joseph have broken if he had yielded to that temptation? What was the source of his strength in resisting?

5. Is Joseph a symbol of Christ in the fact that he was unjustly condemned and punished? Must Christians today also be prepared to suffer for righteousness' sake? (Matt. 5:10-11).

6. The road Joseph had to travel from Potiphar's house to Pharaoh's palace went through the prison. Do you suppose he sometimes wondered about God's providence and doubted His leading? With the hindsight of faith, can we now see how God was working in all these things for the good of His people? Did Joseph later come to see it clearly too? (Gen. 50:19-20). Did he sense it all along?

7. How did Joseph witness to God's Word in prison? Did he give God the glory for giving him the wisdom to interpret dreams? (Gen. 40:8).

8. Was the movement in Joseph's life from humiliation to exaltation a preview of the humiliation leading to exaltation in Christ's work of salvation?

9. What new opportunities and new dangers did Joseph's top-level position in the Egyptian government entail?

10. Explain the significance of Joseph's new name, *Zaphenath-paneah*, that is, "redeemer of the world and preserver of life." Did Pharaoh grasp the full meaning of this name he gave Joseph? Did Joseph perhaps have a hand in this choice of name? Do you suppose he related it in his mind to the plight of his father and brothers back in Canaan? Did he often think of them? Did he relate his own life to their future well-being? How does this new name reflect God's grand design in bringing Joseph down into Egypt?

11. God's basic purpose in Joseph's life was to make him a blessing to the covenant community and—through them—to the world. Is that also God's purpose with our lives? How can we begin to live up to that purpose?

# 33: Restored Unity

*Genesis 42-45*

1. Does a Bible story like this ever bring tears to your eyes? Tears of spiritual relief and overwhelming joy? Tears of holy envy, a deep-seated desire for such soul-satisfying experiences of forgiveness, reconciliation, and rediscovered unity?

2. Isn't restored unity, the theme of this chapter, exactly what was lacking in the lives of those patriarchs all along? Isn't it just what we have been hoping and looking for in the family life of Abraham, Isaac, and Jacob?

3. How was this episode God's crowning act in Joseph's life, allowing him to see the realization of what he had believed during all those long years of separation, namely, that he was chosen and prepared by God to be the preserver of his people?

4. What made it possible for Joseph to brush aside all thoughts of revenge upon the wrongdoings of his brothers? Is such a spirit still possible today? (Rom. 12:14-21).

5. What is the main point that comes through in this Bible story? Show how the "happy ending" was unmistakably God's doing.

6. Reconstruct the successive steps Joseph followed in allowing this dramatic reunion to unfold in such a masterful way.

7. Why did Joseph test his brothers in such an agonizing way? What was he looking for in their lives? A changed heart? True conversion?

8. How did the following aspects of spiritual renewal come to expression in the brothers' response to Joseph's challenges—a sense of guilt for past crimes, readiness to confess their sins, self-denial and self-sacrifice, an end to the old jealousies and bickering, a new spirit of unity?

9. More specifically, show how these trying events drew out of Jacob a readiness to let everything go in total surrender to the almighty God of the covenant; out of Reuben a witness to the earlier unrighteousness of the brothers; out of Simeon a willingness to be held ransom for his brothers; out of Judah a commitment to lay his life on the line for his younger brother Benjamin; out of Benjamin the courage to accompany his brothers into a very threatening situation.

10. How was Judah's offer to serve as substitute for the safety of his brother a dim and distant prefiguration of the substitutionary atonement of Jesus Christ? Why was this such a fitting act on the part of Judah in the light of the future Messianic role of the tribe of Judah? Are we still called to such acts of self-sacrificing love? (John 15:12-17).

11. How could the Spirit of the Lord Jesus Christ be at work hundreds of years in advance in Joseph and—through Joseph—in the other members of Jacob's household?

12. Once the brothers had demonstrated a new spirit of forgiveness and unity, Joseph repeatedly told them to lay their guilty consciences to rest. Why was this important? How was such a thing possible? Upon what basis can we find a similar peace of mind?

13. How can we account for the fact that this Pharaoh was so eager to welcome these "foreigners," the Hebrews, into the land of Egypt? Could it be, as archeology suggests, because this Pharaoh was himself a "foreigner" and would therefore be more sympathetic than a true Egyptian to other "foreigners"?

14. What was God's purpose in providing a place of refuge for the chosen people in Egypt?

# 34: The Preserver of Life

*Genesis 46-47*

1. Point out how God's revelation concerning Joseph's leadership role, a revelation that came through Joseph's boyhood dreams, had now come true. How did Joseph serve as the preserver of his father's house? How was this a sign and symbol of the work of Christ as Savior of His people?

2. Explain De Graaf's statement that "the people of God are the focal point as the Lord's counsel is fulfilled in the history of the world" (p. 241). How was the well-being of Egypt bound up with the well-being of Israel? Is it still true today that God, in Jesus Christ, shows favor to the unbelieving world for the sake of His people? Did Egypt share indirectly in God's covenant blessings upon the house of Jacob? Do God's blessings upon His people today still spill over into the lives of others?

3. God provided a place for the covenant family in Egypt until they would become large and strong enough to assume an independent place within the land of Canaan. How real was the danger that God's people would mingle with the Canaanites and lose their spiritual identity?

4. How was Israel's assignment to the land of Goshen related to their major occupation, i.e. herding cattle? What was the attitude of the Egyptian people toward shepherds? How were the Israelites assured of the isolation they needed to lead a separate life?

5. Why was Jacob reluctant to leave the land of Canaan to go down to Egypt?

6. Why did Jacob make Joseph promise that he and his brothers would one day bury him in the land of promise? Were the patriarchs breaking all their ties with Canaan? Or did they view their move to Egypt as temporary—a pilgrimage that would eventually lead them back to their fatherland, the land of promise?

7. Is it possible, as De Graaf suggests, to question the wisdom of Joseph's economic-social-political policies in Egypt? Did his programs place too much wealth and power in the hands of Pharaoh? Was he right in moving people from the country into cities? Did he make the people too dependent on the state? Was this development perhaps related to the Egyptian view that their ruler was a god-like figure?

8. Pharaoh, as an unbeliever, viewed this world as his fatherland and the goal of his life. By way of contrast, how did Jacob describe his life in the world as he appeared before the royal court?

9. The patriarchs saw themselves as strangers in the land of Canaan, awaiting their full possession of it. Even then they would still be pilgrims traveling on toward God's final blessing—a new earth under new heavens. In what sense are we as Christians today also called to live in the world as strangers and pilgrims? Egypt meant "not yet" to the Israelites. Does our life also have a "not yet" character to it?

10. In the days of Jacob and Joseph, there was a sharp line of separation between the Israelites and the Egyptians, between Canaan and Egypt, between the land of Goshen and the rest of Egypt. Today, after the coming of Christ and the gift of the Holy Spirit, can we draw similar lines between peoples and places? Or does the gospel go out to all peoples and all places?

11. What does it mean that the only valid antithesis left is between two ways of life—the life of faith and the life of unbelief?

12. Is De Graaf's warning against accepting a dichotomy between the sacred and the secular still necessary today? What does it mean that "to a believer, everything is grace"? If life is all one

piece, how must it then be lived in its entirety? Is the church sacred and the state secular? (p. 242).

# 35: The Bringer of Peace

*Genesis 48-50*

1. What future perspectives did Jacob open up in his prophecies concerning his sons? Were these prophecies fulfilled in one lifetime? How far into the future did they reach?

2. Why is it important that Joseph and his sons wished to be counted among God's covenant people, even though they were part of high-level Egyptian life? Should the same issue weigh heavily upon us too?

3. Joseph received the blessing of the first-born son (a double inheritance) in place of Reuben, who had forfeited his right. May we regard this as God's reward for the prominent role he played as the preserver of Israel's life?

4. In blessing Joseph's two sons, Jacob gave the greater blessing to the younger son, Ephraim, and the lesser blessing to the older son, Manasseh. How was this prophecy fulfilled in Israel's later history? Why was the entire northern kingdom of Israel, the ten tribes who broke away from the house of David, often called *Ephraim*?

5. Jacob bestowed his final will and testament upon his sons one by one (Gen. 49). Does each prophecy give us a good insight into the future role of the son to which it applied? How do you suppose the twelve sons felt as they listened to their father's words?

6. The special covenantal blessing, in which Israel's Messianic hopes were concentrated, came to Judah. What does the central theme of that blessing (i.e. "Shiloh") mean? What was to be Judah's special calling in the unfolding history of the covenant? Was God's choice of Judah based on Judah's personal merits or on God's forward-looking, electing grace? Who were to be some of the personal links in this chain leading from Judah to the

coming Christ? What does the word *Shiloh* tell us about Christ as the Prince of Peace? What does it tell us about the nature of His Kingdom? Is that peace already a reality? Is it still a future hope? Or a combination of both?

# 36: I Am Who I Am

*Exodus 1-4*

1. During the roughly 400 years between the end of the Genesis narrative and the beginning of the Exodus narrative, big changes had taken place among the Israelites in Egypt. Explain these changes in terms of Israel's development from a family into a nation, from weakness to a position of strength, from having arrived as a favored clan to its plight as an enslaved people. How are all these developments summarized in the words "Now there arose a new king over Egypt, who did not know Joseph"? (Ex. 1:8).

2. How can De Graaf argue that the central event in the book of Exodus is the re-establishment of the covenant with Israel as a nation at Mount Sinai? Was the exodus event a means in God's hand, a means leading to this climactic end? Or do the exodus and Mount Sinai go hand in hand as companion events?

3. How is it apparent from all the events surrounding the exodus that the decisive issue was whether Israel was to be a free people belonging to God or an enslaved people belonging to Pharaoh?

4. As we reflect on Israel's hardships in Egypt, why should we place the emphasis not on Pharaoh's acts of persecution but on God's judgments and blessings in the life of His covenant people? How was God active in this program of oppression, testing and purifying and redeeming Israel? Is it clear that Israel's continued existence was dependent solely on God's preserving and intervening grace?

5. How did the decree to wipe out all male children among the Israelites pose a severe threat to the very survival of Israel as a separate people? What results would widespread intermarriage

have led to? Would such mingling with the Egyptians have destroyed the covenantal identity of God's chosen people?

6. What were the radical differences in religion between the Egyptians and the Israelites? After 400 years in Egypt, was Israel's worship and service of God still true and holy?

7. Was the act of faith by Moses' parents in saving the boy's life (Heb. 11:23) also an act of civil disobedience? Must believers always obey their rulers? Must they sometimes resist and disobey? Is it true that when rulers act justly, we must obey them—for God's sake—but when they act unjustly, we must disobey them—also for God's sake?

8. How can we account for Moses' decision, despite his heavy involvement in the highest circles of Egyptian social life, not to join the Egyptians but to side with his downtrodden fellow Israelites and take up their cause? Was this an act of faith? Was this act motivated by a future vision of God's blessing upon the Hebrews through the promised Messiah? (See Hebrews 11:24-8 and Acts 7:17-34.)

9. Explain the following purposes involved in God's calling of Moses:
   a) To serve as a mediator between God and Israel,
   b) to act as Israel's head before God,
   c) to be the leader in escaping Egypt, and
   d) to be God's spokesman in re-establishing the covenant at Mount Sinai.

In which ways did Moses serve as a type and symbol of the coming Christ?

10. What lessons of leadership did Moses have to learn during his exile in Midian?

11. How did that encounter at the burning bush mark a crucial turning point in Moses' life? Is it understandable that Moses should shrink back from the awesome office of mediator to which God called him? How did God overcome his excuse? What assurance did God give Moses that His Word would not fail?

12. In future events, how did the rod in Moses' hand represent God's presence and His mighty acts of deliverance?

13. Why was it important for Moses, as a mediator of the covenant,

to comply with the covenantal sign of circumcision before proceeding to serve as the leader of the covenant people in their freedom march out of Egypt? How important are the signs and seals of the covenant, i.e. circumcision and the Passover in the Old Testament, baptism and the Lord's supper today?

14. Is it understandable that the people of Israel should accept Moses' leadership with mixed feelings—at first with enthusiasm and later with bitter grumbling? Did they understand the real intent of his mission, namely, to renew the covenant? Or were they only driven by the urge to escape bondage?

# 37: Freedom to Serve the Lord

*Exodus 5-11*

1. Point out how this struggle in Egypt was taking place at various levels of encounter—Moses versus Pharaoh, the Israelites versus the Egyptians, Yahweh versus the gods of the land.

2. In what sense did this struggle involve the sovereign rights of God as ruler of the nations and Lord of all? What were God's rights over Egypt? What were His very special rights over Israel?

3. Explain De Graaf's main thought running through this chapter, namely, that Israel's freedom to serve the Lord was at stake. Was this the issue that is now called "freedom of worship"? Why does God insist on the basic human right to worship and serve Him freely? Are there other cases of violation of this freedom in the Old Testament? (See I Kings 12:28-30 and Daniel 6:6-9.) And in the New Testament? (See Acts 4:13-22.) Do Christians— ourselves and others—still experience violations of "religious liberty" today?

4. What does it mean that Pharaoh was to be a guardian over Israel's life? Did this hold for the other peoples in Egypt too? Is that the God-given task of all rulers? How are we to understand the government's calling to safeguard the religious freedom and basic rights of all people within its borders? What does it mean that governmental authority is under God? (John 19:10-11).

How is that authority to be exercised for the good of the people?

5. How are we to understand that twofold Biblical teaching that God hardened Pharaoh's heart, on the one hand, while Pharaoh hardened his own heart against God and His people, on the other? Is it true that God raised up Pharaoh in order to demonstrate His glory and power in Egypt? (Rom. 9:17). Is it also true that Pharaoh repeatedly chose freely to oppose God's will for Israel? (Ex. 5:1-4). May we play the one truth off against the other? How can we keep both sides of the truth in Biblical balance?

6. Read and reflect on Psalm 105:23-42 as a poetic commentary on the exodus event.

7. Describe the mounting intensity and growing severity of the first nine plagues. Notice how the plagues struck closer and closer to home in the lives of the Egyptians—first at the land, then at all nature, then directly at the people themselves. Why did God cause the Israelites to share in the sufferings of the first plagues? Why did God later distinguish between Israel and Egypt by shielding the Israelites from His more drastic judgments?

8. How are we to understand such miracles as Moses' rod turning into a serpent? Are miracles simply displays of raw power? Or are they signs of God's judgment and grace? Are they automatic proofs of God's reality and presence? Or does it require faith to recognize God's hand in miracles?

9. Is it possible for people like Pharaoh to reject God's claim so long and hard that they reach a point of no return? Do they then place themselves beyond repentance? Do they remove themselves from God's mercy? Do they make themselves ripe for judgment? Are God's judgments in the world today too? Do we recognize God at work in them? Are people responding to them by turning back to God? Or do we, like modern Pharaohs, view God's judgments as unfortunate accidents to be explained by natural causes?

# 38: Resurrection

*Exodus 12—13:16*

1. During that memorable night in Egypt, God set the Israelites apart unto life and the Egyptians unto death. Was that because the Israelites were better and holier? Didn't the Israelites deserve to sink into the same grave of death and destruction as the Egyptians? Upon what basis were they given a new lease on life? In what sense was their deliverance a resurrection? How is Easter the fulfillment of Israel's Passover?

2. At the heart of this exodus event was the Passover feast, which was laden with symbolic meaning. Explain the symbolism involved in these various aspects of that meal:
   a) the whole lamb without a broken bone
   b) the unleavened bread
   c) the bitter spices
   d) eating as households
   e) standing to eat, ready to travel.

3. The Passover, coming centuries after circumcision, became Israel's second sacrament. What does each of these sacraments stand for? How are they related to each other? What form do these two sacraments take in the New Testament church? Does something of their original Jewish meaning live on in our present Christian sacraments of baptism and the Lord's supper?

4. How were the elements of sacrifice and sacrament, atonement and celebration, combined in the Passover feast? Which one of the two is basic to the other? Are these two elements also present in the Lord's supper? Which predominates?

5. How did the blood of the lamb sprinkled on the doorposts serve as a sign of the saving work of the coming Christ?

6. What did the first-born in Israel stand for? How could the first-born represent the whole family or the whole nation? What was the lot of Egypt's first-born? Of Israel's first-born? What did it mean in later Israelite history that the first-born in every family, the first-born of the flocks, and the first fruits of the harvest were to be dedicated to God? Did those acts sym-

bolize the consecration of the whole of life to God's service? Does this still hold true for our tithes?

7. Why were the Egyptians so eager to give their possessions to the fleeing Hebrews? Was it right of Israel to accept these "gifts" and thus plunder Egypt?

8. De Graaf speaks of a "mixed multitude" that accompanied Israel in the exodus (p. 277). Who were these people? Were they people who wanted to escape bondage and destruction in Egypt? Were they people who had become relatives of the Israelites through intermarriage? How could they become full-fledged members of the covenant community? Did the presence of this "mixed multitude" point ahead to many other "outsiders" who would later be incorporated into the people of God, such as Rahab and Ruth? Did it point ahead to the Gentiles of New Testament times and the Christian community around the world today, which is also a "mixed multitude"?

# 39: The Day of the Lord

*Exodus 13:17—15:21*

1. The words of this chapter title are sprinkled across the pages of the Bible, both Old Testament and New, especially in the prophets and in the fulfillment of their prophecies in the gospel of Jesus Christ. What is the basic meaning of this title? How does that meaning fit the exodus event? Did the day of the Lord come all at once in a single event, or in a series of successive events? On those days of the Lord, did God reveal His judgment or His grace, His glory or His love, or all the various aspects of His relationship to the world? In what sense was the coming of Christ the central and decisive day of the Lord? Which day of the Lord is still to come?

2. How is Pharaoh's sin of hardening his heart symptomatic of the sins of all mankind?

3. How does the Red Sea, separating Israel from Egypt represent

the separation of believers and unbelievers throughout the history of the world? How does it serve as a sign pointing to the meaning of baptism?

4. In taking the bones of Joseph with them, the Israelites were not just keeping a promise made long before to father Joseph; they were also actively confessing their faith. What were they proclaiming by this deed?

5. Be sure to consult a Bible atlas or map to get a clear picture of Israel's route out of Egypt. Why did God lead them along this strange, roundabout way? Why the detour? Why avoid Philistine country? Why in the direction of the Red Sea? Why, beyond that, toward Mount Sinai?

6. What did the cloudy-fiery pillar represent in Israel's journeys? Was it a sign of judgment, or blessing, or both? How was this divine pointer, too, fulfilled in Jesus Christ?

7. What was God teaching His people when He led them into a trap at the shores of the Red Sea? How did they respond to this predicament? How did Moses react? How did God come through to deliver His people?

8. Is it true, as De Graaf says, that we cannot "explain" the Red Sea crossing? (p. 283). Does the blowing of the east wind all night tell the whole story? Or must we sing the song of Moses (Ex. 15) in order to sense the secret of this mind-boggling event?

9. The bottom line to Israelite-Egyptian relationships is that "separation for all time" (p. 283). There is an awful finality to those words. Can such language also be used in connection with God's last judgment upon the world?

10. Throughout this chapter, De Graaf repeatedly says that God's judgment upon Pharaoh and his hosts is a dramatic demonstration of God's love claiming its rights. How are we to bring God's love and His rights together? Doesn't love mean giving up one's rights? Or does God have a right to our love? And if that right is spurned, does love then descend in judgment?

11. How does Moses' song of victory (Ex. 15), sung by Israel upon reaching the other side of the Red Sea, point ahead to the final triumph of believers in the midst of tribulation as they sing the

song of Moses and the Lamb? (Rev. 15:1-4).

# 40: Borne on Eagles' Wings

*Exodus 15:22—17:16*

1. During that hard three-month trek from the Red Sea to Mount Sinai, the Israelites wavered constantly between their new freedom in the Lord and the old security of Egypt. Though they had left the land of Egypt behind, was the spirit of Egypt still too much with them?

2. Marah was the place of bitter waters. Was it also the place of bitter experiences? Is it understandable that Israel should be so quick to tempt God and complain against Moses—or is it disappointing? How did God reveal Himself there as Israel's healer? Did Moses' use of a piece of wood to cure the waters (rather than his famous staff) arise out of a desire to resist notions of magic which the people had taken with them from Egypt?

3. How was Israel's ingratitude reflected even in the name *Manna*? What was God teaching His people by supplying food one day at a time? Do we today realize what we are asking when we pray: "Give us this day our daily bread"? How did God punish those Israelites who tried to hoard manna? How did Jesus relate His coming into the world to His Father's gift of manna? (John 6:31-5).

4. What was the purpose of the sabbath in Israel's life? What is the importance of the fact that Israel observed the sabbath even before the sabbath law was given on Mount Sinai? Does the sabbath go back to creation? In giving manna, how did God provide sabbath rest for His people? What happened to those Israelites who treated the sabbath like any other day when it came to gathering manna?

5. At Rephidim the Israelites again provoked God and rebelled against Moses. How did God respond to their hard-heartedness—by rising up in righteous anger or by stooping

humbly as a servant to meet their needs? Did striking the rock to bring forth water lead Israel to true repentance?

6. Don't you marvel at the patience and enduring love of the Lord in putting up with the stubborn Israelites, providing for their needs, forgiving their sins, and receiving only thankless complaints in return? Are *we* any better?

7. The prophets picture these wanderings in the wilderness as the courtship years between God as the groom and Israel as His bride. Entering Canaan would then be entering the marriage state. What kept the engagement going during that stormy period of courtship—God's faithfulness, or Israel's? What does this teach us about the covenant of grace?

8. Along the way, Israel was called upon to fight its first battle. What was so shameful about the attacks made by the Amalekites, who were descendants of Esau? Was this another round in the old enmity between Esau and Jacob? How were Moses' upheld arms a sign of the real source of victory? Why was Israel instructed never to make peace with the Amalekites? How did the first major attempt to wipe them out end in failure? (I Sam. 15:1-23). How did a further battle lead to the defeat of the Amalekites? (I Sam. 30:1-20). How did the hostilities between Israel and Amalek end? (I Chron. 4:43).

9. How does the title of this chapter aptly describe God's way with Israel in the wilderness? (Ex. 19:4).

# 41:  The Covenant Established

*Exodus 18-24*

1. In what sense was the covenant made at Mount Sinai the central event of all those long, hard years in the wilderness? Was the covenant of grace there established or *re*-established? Was it a *new* covenant or a *renewal* of God's single covenant with His people? The covenant at Mount Sinai was *national*; it was made not with some patriarch and his family but with the nation of Israel. Does this mean it was a brand-new covenant?

2. De Graaf states that in one sense the covenant is *two*-sided, while in another sense it is *one*-sided (p. 295). Explain how the covenant is *one*-sided, coming exclusively from God's side in its divine initiative, owing its origin to a gracious God who makes the first move. Explain how the covenant is also *two*-sided, involving both parties (God *and* His people) in an ongoing relationship of revelation and response, a relationship that takes in both God's promise of redemption and our call to obedient living.

3. How did Moses' priestly act of sprinkling half of the blood on the altar and the other half on the people reflect the two sides of the covenant? How was it a sign of atonement and reconciliaton between God and Israel? Does that spiritual ceremony teach us something about Christ's saving work in the lives of His people?

4. Was the meeting at Mount Sinai just a local Jewish affair? Or was God there reaching out to the whole world *through* Israel? How does that covenant and the law which came with it hold for all men, then and now?

5. Did God choose the Israelites to be His special, chosen covenant people *because* they were so well suited to this end? Or did God's choice, His electing love, *make* them, unworthy and undeserving as they were, into a special people? How was this choice of Israel related to the coming of Christ? Do all Christians today belong to that chosen and special nation of prophets, priests, and kings?

6. How did Moses' role as mediator between God and His people point ahead to the office and work of Christ as Mediator?

7. What important function does the Angel of the Lord repeatedly serve at various points in the unfolding history of the covenant? Does this Angel offer us a preview of God's final revelation of Himself in Jesus Christ?

8. Covenant means close fellowship with God. Yet, how does the Mount Sinai meeting also reveal the majesty and supreme holiness of God? Why did Israel have to keep a proper distance from God? Is reverence for God's sovereignty lacking in Christian faith and life today?

9. When God comes with His law, He comes first in His covenant. When He reveals His will for our lives, He first gives us the grace to obey. How does this come to expression in the introductory words to the ten commandments? Is the covenant always the context for faithfully keeping the law? Where does keeping the law without living in the covenant lead? To legalism? Did this happen often in Israel? Were the Pharisees guilty of legalism? Are there signs of legalism in our lives too?

10. Why did God speak largely in prohibitions and negative commands to ancient Israel? Does the law come to us with a more positive thrust today? How can we account for that?

11. How should the ten commandments function in our lives today? As a teacher of our sins? As a rule for thankful living? As a way to curb sin in society? Are they a summary of all God's many laws for our lives as revealed to Israel and the early church? Is there still an abiding *norm* in the law? Are the ten commandments examples of how to keep the central law of love? Point out how the law of God holds for all our life relationships.

# 42: The Mediator

*Exodus 32-34*

1. Explain as clearly as you can what is involved in the Biblical idea of a mediator. Do mediators sometimes settle differences between people as well as between God and man? What do we think of when we hear about someone mediating a dispute—between labor and management, for example? In what settings have we met Moses as mediator before? Here his mediatorial office comes to clearest expression. How is Christ as Mediator superior to Moses?

2. What was taking place between God and Moses during those forty days?

3.  What was the motivation behind the Israelites' demand for an idol-god—instead of Moses—to lead them? Were they merely rejecting the leadership of Moses, or were they also, and more basically, rejecting God's rule over their lives? Were the Israelites acting like the heathen peoples around them in turning away from the invisible God of the covenant in favor of a god they could see and touch, as though the latter god were more real? How is Egyptian influence evident in the decision to make this image in the form of a calf? What must we think of Aaron's part in this sad spectacle?

4.  Why are images of God so wrong? Did the Israelites intend to worship the image as god or to worship God by means of the image? In other words, were they violating the first commandment or the second—both of which were being etched out in tablets of stone at that very time on the mountain? God forbids making images because He has made His own image—man. What does it mean that we are images of God? (Gen. 1:27). How are we now to understand that Christ is "the image of the invisible God"? (Col. 1:15).

5.  While Moses was still on the mountain, God told him that the Israelites had broken the covenant and that His judgment therefore rested upon them. What arguments did Moses, as mediator, use in pleading with God not to destroy His people? (p. 305). What are we to make of De Graaf's statement that God answered Moses' prayer for Christ's sake?

6.  In what sense were the ten commandments, engraved on those stone tablets, already broken before Moses broke them by dashing them to the ground? Does that law have any meaning apart from the covenant? If the covenant is broken, is the law already broken too?

7.  How did God in His righteousness bring judgment upon His idolatrous people?

8.  The mediator, Moses, in his intercession for his own people, made the ultimate appeal: Destroy me, but save the people! In what sense was this an impossible request for God to honor? How did Paul make a similar appeal? (Rom. 9:1-5). Who was the only one who could rightly die for others?

9.  This passage ends, as it began, with Moses on the mountain,

where the covenant was graciously renewed. Explain how God's promise and our obligations (the demands made on us) are the very heart of the covenant.

# 43: God's Dwelling Place

*Exodus 25-31, 35-40*

1. Trace the idea of God's presence in creation as it binds all of world history together—by answering these questions:
    a) In what sense was all creation originally filled with God's presence?
    b) How did sin alienate the world from God?
    c) How was God's renewed presence among His people symbolized in the tabernacle?
    d) How was it fulfilled in Christ—in principle?
    e) How will it one day be restored in perfection?

2. What can we learn from the fact that the plan and model of Israel's tabernacle originated on the mountain? Was it Moses' idea, or God's? Though it was modeled according to heavenly things, was it still a very earthly structure? What materials went into its construction?

3. What does the involvement of the Israelites, expressed in freewill offerings and donated labor, tell us about their response to this symbol of God's presence in their lives?

4. Describe the Holy of Holies. What did the placement of the ark within it represent? Who could enter it, how often, and for what purpose? Of what was the curtain, which closed it off, a reminder? What happened to the curtain at the time of Christ's crucifixion?

5. What were the contents of the Holy Place? How often did the priests enter it, and for what purpose? What did the daily sacrifices on the great altar represent? Why were the first fruits of the harvest placed on the table of showbread? How did the first fruits represent God's gifts to Israel, given back to God in gratitude? How did the golden lampstand symbolize

Israel's calling to be the light of the world?

6. Who were allowed into the court of the tabernacle? What thoughts were to go through the Israelites' minds as they watched the priests busy with the sacrifice of burnt offerings? Why did the priests have to wash themselves in the large bronze basin before sacrificing?

7. Point out how the various burnt offerings and Israel's involvement in them represented:
   a ) the consecration of their whole life to God
   b ) an atonement for their sins
   c ) fellowship within the believing community.

8. How did the tabernacle picture both God's *presence* with the people of Israel and His *distance* from them? Was the idea of God's presence *fulfilled* in Christ? Was the idea of God's distance *overcome* in Christ?

# 44: Consecrated to God

*Leviticus 8—10:7*

1. How did the sudden way Aaron's two sons were struck down by God serve to impress upon Israel the holiness and earnestness of the priestly office? What seems to have gone wrong? Did God overreact? Did God have a good reason for bringing down gloom over such a joyful day of celebration? What is the ultimate answer to the question Aaron must have asked: Who, then, can be a holy and righteous priest?

2. What made the house of Aaron worthy to serve as priests before the Lord? Were the men of Aaron's family worthy in themselves? Or were they worthy because God had chosen the tribe of Levi as He looked ahead to Christ?

3. What basic differences does the Bible reveal between the priesthood of Aaron and the priesthood of Christ?

4. How is the special office of priest in Israel related to the priestly office to which all men are called by God? How are

the special offices in the church today related to that general priestly office? Is the special office intended to serve the general office of all believers, or vice versa? How was the universal office of all Christians recovered during the Reformation of the sixteenth century? To what priestly tasks does God call all of us today?

5. Describe the priestly garments of Aaron and his sons. What did those garments symbolize?

6. Describe the service of dedication at which the house of Aaron was ordained to the priesthood. What was the spiritual meaning of those various symbolic acts?

7. Almost every aspect of the priestly ministry in Israel is related directly to the redeeming work of Jesus Christ. Is De Graaf therefore justified in his frequent Christ-centered interpretations of those things? Is his interpretation true to Scripture? What light does the book of Hebrews shed on these issues?

# 45: Israel's Calling

*Numbers 9:15—10:36*

1. Reflect on the meaning of Israel's journey through the wilderness in the light of I Corinthians 10:1-13. There Paul says that God's various blessings and judgments came upon Israel as warnings for us, that "they were written down for our instruction." He recalls the supernatural rock which followed Israel through the wilderness, adding that "this rock was Christ!" Paul's interpretation seems to be the model followed by De Graaf in drawing parallels between the life of Israel and the life of the church today. Israel's experience and ours is focused in Jesus Christ. How far may we go in pressing these parallels? Should we be careful, as De Graaf says (p. 327), when we draw these comparisons?

2. What was the true goal of Israel's life during the stay in the wilderness? To leave the wilderness behind and enter Canaan?

Or to serve the Lord first, last, and always—whether in the wilderness or in Canaan? Is living in fellowship with God dependent upon time and place? Could the Israelites rightly postpone that fellowship until they arrived in Canaan? Can *we* put it off until later—until we get to heaven? What does Paul say about the all-controlling principle of our lives, whether in this life or in the life to come? (Rom. 14:7-9; Phil. 1:19-26).

3. How did God govern the *direction* (toward Canaan) and the *tempo* (the stops and starts) of Israel's march? What role did the Angel of the Lord and the cloudy pillar play? How do these two instruments of God's leading hand help to open up the meaning of God's rule in our lives through Jesus Christ?

4. The preaching of the gospel today is often called "the trumpet's joyful sound." Does such language point back to the use of trumpets in Israel? Does the trumpet sometimes also give forth a "threatening sound"? Does it ever call us to active service?

5. The tabernacle symbolized God's dwelling place among His people, Israel. How has this symbol now become reality through the indwelling of the Holy Spirit? (I Cor. 3:16; 6:19; II Cor. 6:16; Eph. 2:21).

6. Moses urged Hobab to join the Israelites, share in their blessings, and exercise his calling for the good of God's people. Is it also our responsibility to constrain men to join the Christian community by saying, "Come with us, share in the good things of the Lord, and discover a worthwhile way to exercise your talents"? Does this gospel call have a more outgoing character in the New Testament era?

7. In leading Israel from one wilderness to another, how was God teaching His people to depend completely on Him?

8. In what way was Israel's life in the wilderness a picture of the Church's present life in the world? Is there a "not yet" element in both? In what way does this parallel *not* hold for the Church in the same manner as for Israel? For Israel, Canaan was still an exclusively future hope. Is our promised Canaan, the coming Kingdom of God, still exclusively future? Or is it—in principle and in part—already a present reality as well as a future hope?

# 46: For His Own Sake

*Numbers 11*

1. The thrust of the title is that God now forgives His people for His own sake. Of course it is true that God always forgives for His own sake, in Jesus Christ. But in this situation there was nothing left for God to do but to forgive apart from the intercession of Moses as mediator, since Moses was powerless to pray. Are the prayers of the righteous on behalf of others important and effective? (James 5:13-18).

2. What were the people of Israel complaining about this time? Didn't they appreciate their freedom from Egyptian bondage? Wasn't fellowship with God a blessing great enough to offset the hardships?

3. Why do you suppose the aliens in Israel were the first to rebel? Were the Israelites themselves open to their unsettling influence? Must we conclude from this incident that "outsiders" are always a threat to God's people?

4. How did the idea of returning to Egypt pose a threat to the covenant people and their calling in the world?

5. Explore the meaning of the last paragraph in De Graaf's section on the people's craving (p. 335).

6. Explain how it was possible for Moses to stand powerless as mediator toward both the people and God. Is it understandable that he concluded that his task was too great for him and that God should relieve him of his responsibilities? In the final analysis, who is the only one who could perform the work of mediator perfectly? Can we say that Christ was also Moses' Mediator?

7. Was God acting justly in sending fire to judge His people and sending quails as a mixed blessing to shame them?

8. How did God's appointment of 70 elders help solve Moses' problems? Was this a means used by God to bring about greater maturity among God's people by spreading responsibility rather than concentrating it all in one man?

# 47: Illegitimate Honor

*Numbers 12*

1. Have you ever thought, for a moment at least, how nice it would be if all those Bible characters (and the rest of God's people too) were good, noble, upright people, if none of this jealousy, pride, and bickering were included in the Bible? But would the Bible then be true to life and honest to God? How do the Bible's exposures of human failure shift the weight of glory to the side of the mighty acts of God's redeeming grace?

2. What was the festering spiritual sore in Miriam's life?

3. What was the occasion in Moses' life which brought this bitter spirit out into the open?

4. What must we think of Aaron for giving in to Miriam's persuasion?

5. De Graaf says that Miriam's basic error was "spiritualism" and "fanaticism" (p. 338). What do these concepts mean?

6. Miriam was driven by the inner impulses of her own heart, while Moses sought to submit himself simply to the Word which came to him from God. Does that account fully for the difference between them in this story? How was Moses like Christ in this respect? Is Miriam's kind of "subjectivism" still a problem today?

7. How did God answer the charges brought against Moses by Miriam? In settling this case, how did God honor Moses before the people of Israel? Was this rebellion against Moses also rebellion against God?

8. How did God's punishment of Miriam bring utter shame and disgrace upon the presumptuous pride of this prophetess? What did leprosy symbolize? What is the point of the comparison that De Graaf draws between Miriam's sentence and the sentence for a woman whose father spit in her face for behaving badly?

9. What does Moses' prayer for Miriam tell us about his role as mediator? Was Moses now in such a spiritual state that he could once again exercise his office? Did God answer his

prayer? How does Moses' intercession point to Christ, who, as Mediator, also takes away our guilt and shame?

# 48:  Light Shining in the Darkness

*Numbers 13-14*

1. How does the title of this chapter, taken from the famous passage about Christ as the Light in the world (John 1), apply here? Did some of the Israelites see Canaan as the land of Light? Very many? Or did most of them walk in darkness? That's what this chapter is about.

2. For the majority in Israel, Canaan was the land of prosperity and luxury, of "milk and honey"—nothing more. For a minority, it was primarily the land of God's inheritance, the land promised to their forefathers, a place to live in peace and righteousness, in covenant fellowship with God and under His rule. What accounts for the difference between these two perspectives? Were both groups eager to possess the land, though for radically different reasons?

3. Is De Graaf right in once again tracing these two opposing viewpoints to *faith*, on the one hand, and *fear*, on the other? Is it true that fear "is always the opposite of faith"? (p. 345).

4. Turning now to the twelve spies, on what were they agreed? On what did they disagree? Did the spies share the same conflicting outlooks as the people? Is it true, as De Graaf says, that "what we see depends on how we look at things"? (p. 345).

5. What conclusions did Israel as a whole draw from the report of the ten spies, first concerning the possibility of entering the land of Canaan, and secondly concerning the possibility of surviving in the wilderness?

6. In reacting to this crisis, what shall we say of their decisions:
   a) to replace Moses with another leader
   b) to return to Egypt

c ) to kill Joshua, Caleb, and the others who, by faith, took their stand upon the promises of God?

7. What does it tell us about Israel that the pleadings of Moses, Aaron, Joshua, and Caleb fell on deaf ears?

8. How did God step in dramatically in His righteous anger and judgment to destroy His people?

9. Moses once again stands as mediator between the offended God and His offending people. Point out how Moses in his intercessory prayer appeals:
    a ) to the covenant promises
    b ) to God's honor among the nations
    c ) to God's gracious power to save His people.
    How did God respond to Moses' pleas?

10. Though God showed mercy, what price did Israel have to pay for its unbelief and rebellion? Do you sense the holy irony in this, that the children, whom the Israelites feared would be destroyed by the giants in Canaan, were the only ones allowed to enter that land? Were the adult Israelites worthy to enter the promised land? Were their children more worthy? Or was entrance into the land of Canaan an act of God's unmerited favor alone?

11. Why did God have to close the doors to Canaan after the frustrated people of Israel decided to go their own way and enter by their own strength? Why is it true that only the Word of God and faith in His covenant blessings can pave the way to the fulfillment of God's promises?

12. Returning now to our first question: Did the Light eventually prevail over the darkness?

# 49: The Head of the People Upheld

*Numbers 16:1-40*

1. Using the light of Scripture, imagine and describe the spiritual climate in Israel during those forty years of aimless wandering in the wilderness. Does such an atmosphere of dejection easily

give rise to evil thoughts of rebellion, such as those of Korah, Dathan and Abiram?

2. What motivated these men and their followers in starting this conspiracy? Why did animosities among the tribes, as well as personal jealousies, always seem to enter into the troubles that arose in Israel? Were these three men trying to make Moses and Aaron scapegoats for all of Israel's problems in the wilderness? What accusations did they bring against God's two appointed leaders?

3. What must we think of their argument that since everybody in Israel was holy unto the Lord, everybody should share in the special services carried out by Moses and Aaron? Was this an appeal to the general office of all believers? Were the three rebels downgrading the special offices, or were they opening them up to all the people? How important is it for us today to have a proper respect for special offices of leadership within the believing community?

4. Why was this plot against Moses actually also a plot against God?

5. What parallel can we draw between the rejection of Moses and the later rejection of Jesus Christ?

6. Was more at stake in this rebellion than the personal positions and prestige of Moses and Aaron? Was God's honor also at stake? And the future development of the covenant line? And the very salvation of the people of Israel?

7. By what test did Moses propose to give the Lord an opportunity to settle the dispute? What happened to these rebels who brought a false offering before the Lord? What conclusion can we draw from the fact that the censers which these men carried were later dedicated to the service of the Lord, while the men themselves were consumed by the anger of the Lord?

8. What was there about the rebellion of Korah, Dathan and Abiram that helps to account for God's devastating judgment upon them? Was it necessary that they be removed from the covenant community with such utter finality?

# 50: A Thriving Priesthood

*Numbers 16:41—17:13*

1. The Bible often speaks of Israel as a stubborn, hardhearted, stiff-necked people. How true! We read that "on the morrow" —the day after witnessing the Korah, Dathan and Abiram disaster—the people again rose up against Moses. That Moses endured these repeated attacks is a testimony to his meekness, patience, and forebearance (Num. 12:3). Can we see in this mediator a preview of the great Mediator?

2. What accusation did the people bring against Moses and Aaron at this time? (Num. 16:41). How was it possible that these two leaders could be blamed for what was so clearly a divine act of judgment? Were the people perhaps implying that Moses and Aaron possessed some sort of evil magical power over Israel?

3. What form did God's judgment upon this further sin of the people take?

4. What is the basis for De Graaf's comment that now there was nothing left to which Moses could appeal before the Lord in defense of his people? (p. 355).

5. Why was the direct intervention of the high priest the only way of escape from the plague? Was Moses right in believing that God would respond in favor to the priestly service which He Himself had instituted in Israel? How could Aaron's action bring about atonement for Israel's sins? Was this possible because of Aaron himself—or because of Christ's priestly atoning work, which was foreshadowed in that of Aaron?

6. What plan did God propose for settling the dispute concerning the legitimacy of Aaron's priesthood? What did those rods symbolize? Why was one rod chosen to represent each of the twelve tribes? What is suggested by this miracle of life from death?

7. Why was Aaron's rod, which budded and bore fruit, given a permanent place in the tabernacle before the ark of the Lord? What important role was this reminder and witness intended to play in Israel's future history?

# 51: The Living God

1. Israel was complaining again about a lack of water—after forty years in the wilderness, with the end of their wanderings in sight. Was the younger generation much better than the older one? Why did they always complain to Moses rather than call upon God for help?

2. Not only did the people express their resentment at having been led out of Egypt, they also declared that they would rather have died with their parents in the wilderness. What does this tell us about their sense of special destiny and future calling?

3. Were they blind to the reality of God—acting as if Moses were the cause of their thirst, rather than seeing that God was behind it? Though they did not deny God, were they pushing Him off into a forgotten corner of their lives? Were they looking upon Moses as if he were God, as if Moses himself had the power to bring about this bad situation and to change it for the good?

4. How can we account for the fact that Moses seems to have given in to this point of view? That he took those complaints upon himself as a personal burden, as if he were indeed God and therefore personally responsible for this situation and personally responsible for finding a way out?

5. When Moses did so, was he being unfaithful to his calling as mediator between God and the people? Was he taking the very place of God instead?

6. To set things straight, God said to Moses: "Honor Me before the people, call upon Me in the presence of the people, and speak to the rock in My name." How would this have let the people know that God's presence was real?

7. What was so serious about Moses' sin of eclipsing God? Of striking the rock in his own strength? Of acting as though he and Aaron could do it on their own? Was this a denial of his office as mediator?

8. If a mediator as great as Moses failed, could any mediator succeed? What did Jesus mean in saying, "I have come down from heaven, not to do my own will, but the will of Him who sent me"? (John 6:38).

9. How did God's act of producing water from the rock bring shame upon Moses as well as the people?

10. What does Paul mean when he says that this rock from which the people drank was Christ? (I Cor. 10:4).

11. How was God glorified in Israel's realization that entrance into Canaan was not even dependent upon such great leaders as Moses and Aaron?

12. Do you suppose the Israelites felt humbled to think that their unbelief was the occasion for keeping Moses and Aaron from entering the promised land?

# 52: Humiliation

*Numbers 20:14—21:9*

1. Consult a Bible atlas or map for a clear picture of the route the Israelites followed in those final stages of their approach to Canaan.

2. The theme running through the four episodes in this chapter is: "Israel humbling itself under the mighty and merciful hand of the Lord." Is the readiness of the Israelites to live in humility before God evidence that at long last a new spirit was beginning to stir among them? In the light of Scripture, show that humility is the response God looks for to the manifestations of His sovereign grace in our lives.

3. What long-standing historical reason was there for Edom's refusal to allow Israel the right to pass through its land? Why did Moses still address Edom as a "brother nation"? (Num. 20:14). Was Israel to respect this special relationship with the descendants of Esau? (Deut. 2:1-8).

4. Did Israel by-pass Edom with a sense of humiliation for

having to back off in the face of Edom's belligerent denial of its brotherly request? Was Edom motivated by pride and self-sufficiency? Did this evil spirit later come under God's judgment? Did the Angel of the Lord also share in Israel's humiliation? How did God later take upon Himself all our humiliation in Jesus Christ?

5. Looking back over Aaron's life, how did he, as Israel's first priest, lay the groundwork for a very large part of Israel's future life? How was he at last humbled for his sin at Meribah? Since Israel's rebellion had led to Aaron's failure to honor God in bringing water from the rock, was Israel as a whole also humiliated by Aaron's death at the very threshold of Canaan? How did God in His grace provide for the continuation of Aaron's priestly ministry? How did the appointment of Aaron's son Eleazar forge another link in the covenant history leading to the coming of the perfect High Priest, Jesus Christ? (Heb. 7:23-8).

6. How did the Israelites' dedication of the spoils of battle taken from Arad demonstrate their willingness to reject self-seeking interests and humbly sacrifice their goods to the Lord? Was a new spirit of obedient service arising in Israel?

7. But just when things are looking up, we hear the same old complaints about water again. Why was water so frequently the crucial test of faith for Israel?

8. Is there, nevertheless, cause for hope even in this new spiritual setback? Why was it a good sign that the Israelites asked Moses to pray to the Lord for them? Did they recognize God as the source of testing and blessing in their lives? Were they willing to humble themselves under Moses as God's appointed mediator?

9. In the midst of God's judgment of death among His people, why was it appropriate that the sign of His healing mercy should take the form of a serpent? Did this bronze serpent itself possess the power to cure the deadly poison in Israel? What did this bronze serpent symbolize? How did it later become a source of idolatry in Israel? (II Kings 18:4). How did this happening in the wilderness find its fulfillment in Christ? (John 3:14-15).

# 53: Blessed by the Lord

*Numbers 21:10—24:25*

1. Is there any evidence that rumors were circulating among the neighboring peoples about God's mighty acts in Israel's life? How did the heathen nations react to the almost incredible reports?

2. Why did God lead Israel to by-pass the land of Moab (as with Edom earlier) and avoid a confrontation with the Moabites?

3. How can we account for the fact that Balaam had some knowledge of the true God? Did it come to him along with reports concerning Israel? Or was it left over from the original knowledge of God from the beginning of history? Or did it perhaps spill over from the revelations which came earlier to the patriarchs? Or had God revealed it to him directly?

4. Describe how Baalam was torn between practicing pagan superstition, magic and fortune-telling, on the one hand, and following the path of true religion by obeying God's Word, on the other hand. How can we account for the fact that many people nowadays are also being led away from true religion to dependence upon occult powers?

5. What was the immediate political reason for Balak's intense fear of Israel? Was there also a deeper spiritual reason for the hatred of Israel which Balak shared with the leaders of other surrounding nations?

6. Why did Balak go to such great lengths to place a curse upon Israel? Did he attach a special importance to such a spoken curse? Was a curse regarded simply as an empty sound, an audible vibration, wishful thinking? Or did Balak, and people generally at that time, believe that whenever a prophet cursed someone, a curse actually struck that person?

7. What basis is there for thinking that Balaam's deepest intent at first was to seek personal gain and advantage in the form of profit, like any other greedy sorcerer? Did he keep on hoping against better knowledge that a way might be found to pronounce a curse, so that he could collect his reward?

8. How did God intervene in Balaam's life to make sure that Israel would be blessed instead of cursed? Did He do so because Israel deserved the blessing more than other peoples, or because He wanted to be true to His covenant promise in choosing Israel, in order to work out His plan of salvation through Israel?

9. Were the sacrifices of Balak and Baalam offered to the God of Israel? Is it possible to sort out clearly the elements of pagan worship and true religion mixed together in the words and deeds of Baalam and Balak?

10. How did the Word of God win out over both Balak and Baalam? God always has the "last word." How did this come through forcefully in Baalam's fourth and final prophecy? (Num. 24:10-25).

11. Pay special attention to Numbers 24:17. Does this prophecy speak of the coming Messiah? Does it have a direct bearing on the words of the magi (like Baalam, wise men from the East) in Matthew 2:2?

12. Is God's Word effective? Is His Word of blessing just a sound that fills the air? Or can we be sure that when God blesses a people, that blessing actually settles upon them?

13. Now, at long last, the Israelites were beginning to tread the soil of the promised land. Can you imagine how they must have felt about that? Did the people tend to view the Transjordan territory, where they were now encamped, as more important or less important than the land of Canaan lying beyond the Jordan?

## 54: The Sovereignty of God's Justice

*Numbers 25-36*

1. We hear a lot of sermons and songs about God's great love. But what about His justice? Do these Bible stories about God's just punishment of evildoers make us feel uneasy?

What do you think of the thesis that God loves justice?

2. Are we so accustomed to injustice in our world that we become calloused to God's strict and sovereign demand for justice? Politicians are all crooked. All businessmen cheat. Everybody cuts corners. Has our sense of righteous indignation and just judgment so eroded that we almost rebel against God's firm insistence on justice as presented in this chapter?

3. Balaam had failed to bring down a curse upon Israel. What new plan did he devise to bring about Israel's downfall?

4. Why was Israel's double wickedness (adultery and idolatry going hand in hand) so serious? Why was it an attack upon Israel's very reason for existence?

5. Why were the heads of Israel so severely punished? Were they primarily responsible for Israel's fall into sin? Does God expect greater faithfulness from those who are called to be the leaders of His people?

6. Why did God constantly remind Israel later of what happened at Baal-Peor, as a warning against this hideous sin and His awful judgment upon it? (Deut. 4:3; Ps. 106:28-31; Hos. 9:10).

7. What did the census reveal about the total number of able-bodied men over twenty years of age in Israel? (Num. 26:1-4, 51). What does this suggest as to the total population of Israel? Could the Hebrew word translated in most Bibles as *thousand* perhaps have some different meaning? Check this point in a recent Bible dictionary.

8. To whom did the promised land of Canaan really belong? How is this reflected in the fact that God divided the land among the tribes according to size by means of casting lots? Given what we know about the ever-present rivalries among the tribes of Israel, does it seem likely that a fair division of the land could have been achieved peaceably by any other means?

9. How was God's command to appoint cities throughout the land for the Levites a constant reminder that all of life in Canaan was to be dedicated to serving Him?

10. How was Joshua chosen as Moses' successor? How did this manner of appointment again reflect God's sovereign rule over Israel?

11. Why did God order such drastic retribution upon the Midianites? How does Baalam again enter Israel's history at this point? How was Israel called to honor God's claim upon its life even in dealing with the spoils of battle?

12. Were the Israelites spared their just punishment because they deserved it? Why then?

13. Why does God demand vengeance upon those who kill their fellow men? Why was the land of promise to be free of the guilt of spilled blood? What role were the cities of refuge to play in protecting the rights of those who unintentionally took human life? How was this system of justice intended to work?

14. How does the pardon granted to refugees when the holder of the office of high priest died point forward symbolically to the work of Christ as the great High Priest?


# 55: The Word Is Very Near You

*Deuteronomy 29-34*

1. To catch the central thrust of this chapter, read carefully Deuteronomy 30:11-14. What does it mean that God's Word is very near, in our hearts and mouths? Must we search for it, high and low, near and far, as though it came as a reward for our hard efforts? Or does God bring it inescapably close to us, reflecting His initiative and grace? Can we say that the Word is the way God is present with us in the world—in creation, in Scripture, and in Christ?

2. Why is this fifth book of Moses called *Deuteronomy*, i.e. "the second law"? (Compare Deuteronomy 5 with Exodus 20.) Why does it give such a prominent place to Moses' farewell address?

3. Why was it appropriate at that point in Israel's history for

Moses to place such strong, repeated emphasis on God's faith-fulness in renewing the covenant with His people?

4. Explain how in these parting words Moses turns the eyes of Israel both backwards and forwards. What was he pointing to in the past? In the future?

5. God's Word is a "two-edged sword," cutting both ways. How is this evident from both the blessings and the curses Moses pronounced? Did Israel need those solemn warnings? Now that the Word incarnate has come, how do Moses' words apply to us?

6. We hear the law of God, in one form or another, every week in church. Yet Moses instructed the priests to read it to Israel every *seven years*! Does it surprise you that this was to be done so infrequently? Were there other ways in which Israel would be confronted with the law day by day?

7. Why did Christ and the apostles view the law of Moses as the very heart of Old Testament revelation? (Matt. 5:17; 11:13; Luke 16:17; Acts 13:15; Rom. 10:4; Gal. 6:2).

8. Show how Moses fulfilled his office as mediator to the very end. How was the Spirit of Christ speaking through him?

9. Give evidence of the universal outlook in Moses' parting speech, the outlook that sees the nations of the world as sharing in Israel's covenant blessings.

10. Isaiah and Peter declared: "All flesh is as grass, but the word of the Lord abides forever." Did these words hold for Moses too? Did the Word of the covenant outlive him? Does that Word now abide forever in Christ, the Word made flesh?

11. Was Moses' mountain-top view of the promised land a good substitute for his failure to enter it?

12. What was unusual about Moses' death? Does it remind you of Elijah's death? Why were these two Old Testament figures the ones to appear on the Mount of Transfiguration?

# 56: Brought into Canaan

*Joshua 1—5:12*

1. After about 500 years of exile, the Israelites were now about to re-enter the land of their forefathers. Compare this new nation of Israel with the family clan which had left centuries before. Describe the internal changes in Israel's life which had taken place during the intervening years.

2. The Bible tells us that God would *give* Canaan to His people. Yet Israel also had to *take* the land as a possession. How are these statements, taken together, related as two sides of the same truth?

3. In what sense was Christ symbolically present in Israel's experience of entering the promised land? Was He present in the directing power of the Angel of the Lord? Was He present in how the ark of the Lord led the way? In the spiritual meaning of the Jordan crossing?

4. Why shouldn't we view the crossing of the Jordan, as gospel hymns sometimes do, as God's act of bringing us from this life into the life to come in heaven? How are we to interpret Israel's deliverance from Egypt and passage through the waters of the Jordan into the land of promise as a Biblical picture of our deliverance from sinful bondage—a deliverance through water leading to fellowship with God and kingdom living?

5. What reasons can we offer for Israel's failure to keep the sacrament of circumcision during those forty years in the wilderness? Does this failure indicate that something was missing in their lives? Why was it important to observe this sacrament as a first act upon entering the land of Canaan?

6. What did the celebration of the Passover mean for the Israelites at this point in their history?

7. How was Joshua's task as leader of Israel different from Moses' task? Where was he to seek his strength in carrying out his task? How did Israel respond to Joshua's leadership?

8. How was the element of surprise present in God's appointed

*timing* for Israel's crossing of the Jordan?

9. Was Rahab's helpfulness to the spies an act of treason, or great courage, or fear, or faith? (Heb. 11:31). Did her decision involve a deeply religious choice on her part?

10. How did Rahab's words reflect the fact that the Spirit of the Lord was going ahead of Israel into the land of Canaan? Is it true, then, that Canaan was being conquered by the fear of the Lord? What more did Israel have to do but follow God's leading?

11. What does the Bible intend to teach us when it points to the central role of the ark in the crossing of the Jordan?

12. What was the purpose of that pile of twelve stones in the Jordan riverbed? What about the twelve stones at the camp in Gilgal? (Josh. 4:5-7, 21-4).

13. Why did the Israelites no longer receive manna once they had entered the promised land?

# 57: Set Apart to the Lord by the Ban

*Joshua 5:13—8:35*

1. What was the meaning of the ban in Israel? Is it the judgment side of the covenant? How did it apply to Israel? How did it apply to the other peoples? May we pronounce the ban over others? Or is this God's right alone?

2. How could something that had been placed under the ban still be sanctified for use by God's people? How is this made clear in the case of the goods taken by Israel at Jericho? What are the implications of the fact that for Christians God has now lifted the ban upon the world? To what end are we to use the world's goods?

3. Is there ample evidence that the peoples of Canaan were ripe for God's ban?

4. What does the presence of the Angel of the Lord (the Com-

mander of the hosts of heaven) and His message to Joshua tell us about the real power behind the conquest of Canaan? Why did Israel still have to become actively involved in this program of conquest? Who was this Angel?

5. At the conquest of Jericho, what was the symbolic religious meaning of:
   a) the presence of the ark of the Lord
   b) the blowing of the trumpets
   c) Israel's silent march around the city?

6. Why was Jericho to remain an open city, never to be rebuilt? What curse would rest upon anyone who disobeyed this edict? Did Joshua's solemn words of warning ever come true? (I Kings 16:34).

7. Why was Israel's defeat at Ai such a serious matter? What was the cause of this defeat? How was the evil cause of this ban removed from Israel? Was this a just punishment on Achan's household?

8. Consult a Bible map to see how the victories at Jericho and Ai opened the way for Israel into the central section of Canaan.

9. How was the covenant renewed at the assembly of Israel at Ebal and Gerizim? Was this renewal ceremony Israel's act of obedience to a command which Moses had given? (Deut. 27:1-8). Describe the scene at the assembly. How are the two sides of the law, blessing and curse, related to each other? How is keeping the law related to keeping the covenant?

# 58: The Righteousness of God

*Joshua 9-12*

1. Reflect upon this key sentence as a clue to the meaning of the entire chapter: "By the hand of Israel, God had executed His righteousness upon the Canaanites" (p. 410).

2. In all these bloody battles, why is it important to keep the righteousness of God clearly in mind as the basic motivation

behind Israel's actions? What if we were to allow human sentiments to become the overriding consideration? Is sparing human life the highest norm in human relationships? Must these acts of divine judgment be seen in the light of Israel's very special place in the history of redemption? Why may we not look to the nations around us today to follow Israel's example?

3. What motivated the Gibeonites in their act of clever deception? What was Joshua's mistake in dealing with their request? Once the deception was uncovered, why was Israel still obligated to grant the Gibeonites protection? What sentence did Joshua impose upon these sly deceivers? How was this sentence a fulfillment of Noah's prophecy upon Canaan? (Gen. 9:25). How were the rights of the Gibeonites later violated and then rectified? (II Sam. 21:1-6).

4. What was the importance of an oath in Israel? In whose name were oaths sworn? Was God's righteousness at stake in Israel's keeping of the oath to the Gibeonites? Did the Gibeonites, too, have certain God-given human rights, rights which Israel had to honor?

5. What basic truth did the Israelites have to learn from living with the Gibeonites? That they themselves were no better? That God does not allow for revenge born of passionate anger? That the destruction of the other Canaanites was justifiable only on the basis of the righteousness of God? That the preservation of Israel was rooted only in the grace of God?

6. How is Christ the ultimate revelation of the righteousness of God? Can this righteousness be earned? Or is it freely given?

7. In what sense was the alliance of the southern cities against the Gibeonites also an alliance against Israel?

8. Do we, as twentieth century scientific people, find it easy to believe in such miracles as God's raining hailstones upon His enemies and giving Israel a long day to gain the full victory? Why do some people seek natural explanations for such events? Just what is a miracle anyway?

9. What is the importance of the spiritual support which God constantly gave Joshua in the words "Be strong and of good

courage"?

10. What seems to have been Joshua's strategy for conquering Canaan? Divide and conquer by first taking possession of the central country, then the south, and finally the north? After these campaigns, was the resistance of the Canaanites broken? Were all the Canaanites then wiped out?

## 59: The Heritage of the Saints

*Joshua 13-22*

1. History books tell us: "To the victors belong the spoils." The Bible, however, tells a different story. Israel was not to view its inheritance of the land as the spoils of battle. It was a gift of the Lord, who allotted to each tribe its portion by casting lots. How does this reveal God's hand in the settling of Canaan? Did these divisions follow the lines laid out in old father Jacob's prophecy? (Gen. 49).

2. Why did the tribe of Simeon lose its independent place, living instead in the shadow of Judah?

3. What was the intended significance of the presence of the Levites scattered in various cities throughout the land?

4. What was the relationship between the special service of the Lord at the central sanctuary and the general service of the Lord to which each Israelite was called in his own inherited tract of land? Was there a sharp separation between the two? Is there still a sharp separation today between serving God in church, on the one hand, and serving Him at home, at school, in our civic life, and in our daily work, on the other? Is such a separation healthy? How will any such separation come to an end on the new earth? (Rev. 21:1-2, 22-7).

5. Dividing the promised land among the tribes of Israel was a final task assigned to Joshua by Moses. When Joshua carried out this task, how was he acting as a mediator? After completing this work, Joshua retired to his own inheritance. What

was Joshua saying to Israel by this act of withdrawing from public life?

6. The land given to the Israelites was a *gift* of God. Yet, they had to *struggle* to gain full possession of it. How can it be that God *gives* it, but Israel must *lay hold* of it? (Phil. 3:12-14.)

7. The Canaanites were not yet completely removed from the land. Was the failure to get rid of them a weakness on Israel's part? What were the results of their continued coexistence among the Israelites? Each tribe was to finish the job in its own territory. Why were the Israelites so slow to take full possession of the land? Why was Jerusalem left unconquered? When was it finally annexed to Israel? How did Caleb's example in claiming his inheritance instil courage in other Israelites? What was his basis for staking his claim?

8. When the two and a half tribes returned to their own land across the Jordan, why did they erect that altar called *Ed*, meaning *witness*? They were immediately suspected of breaking the bond of unity in Israel. Was this suspicion justified? To what were they witnessing? What does this everpresent spirit of misunderstanding and mistrust tell us about the spiritual state of affairs among the twelve tribes? The Transjordan tribes feared that they would be viewed as second-class citizens in Israel. Why was the preservation of unity in Israel so important?

# 60: Confirmed in the Inheritance

*Joshua 23-24*

1. Joshua's final act was to renew the covenant. Does this remind you of the way Moses also closed his career? Describe how Joshua, like Moses, served as mediator between God and His people in his last two meetings with the Israelites. In what sense was Joshua a type of the coming Mediator, Jesus Christ? How was he speaking for the coming Christ and acting in His strength?

2. Two points stand out in Joshua's farewell speech—assurance and warning. How does Joshua *assure* the Israelites of God's covenant faithfulness? Were they to see their inheritance in the land as a confirmation of that faithfulness? What blessings would be theirs if they lived in obedience before the Lord? What did Joshua say in *warning* Israel about the danger of mingling with the Canaanites and adopting their life-style? What threats of judgment did he hold out to them as the fruits of disobedience? Did his warning already carry with it the thought that if they turned away from God, they would be taken out of their land? (Remember what happened to Israel centuries later—deportation and exile.)

3. The Canaanites were a constant source of temptation to the Israelites. How had this been true in the past? How would it prove to be true in the future? How can we account for the seductive power of the Canaanites over the Israelites when it came to marriage and worship? Was it because of their more advanced methods of farming? Or their highly developed culture? Or their superior system of building towns? (Remember, the Israelites had been a wandering people.) Or the sex acts connected with their idol worship? Is there still a real danger of accommodating ourselves to ungodly life-styles today?

4. Farewell speeches in Israel, like the two made by Joshua, seem to have been lengthy recollections of the nation's history as a people of God from the time of the patriarchs to the present. Think ahead to Stephen's farewell speech (Acts 7). Why was national history so important to Israel? Was it told to build up national pride? Or to recount the mighty acts of God? Did Israel have a different view of history than the other peoples? The heathens viewed history as going round in circles; Israel viewed history as moving from the past, through the present, toward a future goal. What goal?

5. Did Joshua confront the Israelites with an easy choice? Or did he put it to them as forcefully as possible—as an all-or-nothing decision? What does De Graaf mean in applying this to our lives with these words: "The Lord is either everything to you or nothing"? (p. 422).

6. How did Joshua offer leadership to Israel in making his own decision? Where did he gain the strength to take such a stand?

7. What was the solemn effect of Joshua's recording this renewal of the covenant in the presence of the people and his erecting a stone as a witness to the people's decision?

8. How did Joshua's death, and the deaths of his contemporaries, mean the breaking of a final link with Israel's past? In what sense was his burial also a sign of his link with the promised land and its future destiny? Was it also a symbol of his faith in the coming resurrection?

9. Explain the meaning of these lines from De Graaf: "Scripture is the book for the earth. The Bible views the earth in the light of heaven, of course, but it remains the book for the earth. Our portion on this earth, in the here and now, is a guarantee of our portion on the earth when it is renewed one day" (p. 419). How was this truth reflected in Joshua's life and death? How was it to come to expression in Israel's future history? How was it revealed centrally in Christ? What difference should it make in our lives?